Unraveled to Unrivaled

Embracing the Four Dimensions of Resilience™

BY JERRY LERNER, MD

© 2023 Jerry Lerner, MD

All rights reserved. Except as permitted under the U.S. Copyright Act of 1976, no part of this publication may be reproduced, distributed, or transmitted in any form or by any means or stored in a database or retrieval system, without the prior written permission of the publisher.

Any registered trademarks referenced in this book
are the property of their respective owners.

Printed in the United States of America

Publisher: Compaire Consulting

First Edition: 2023

ISBN: 979-8-218-23732-5

This book is dedicated to the three amazing women at the center of my life and heart— my daughters, Arielle Weber and Geneva Lerner, and my wife and partner, Stephanie Sikes. You have all demonstrated amazing courage and resilience in the face of your adversities and challenges— all with love, integrity, and humor. I cherish your wonderful spirits in my life.

"A patient once said to me, 'Doctor, I hurt all over; my body is aching, I'm in great emotional turmoil, and my very soul feels damaged beyond all repair. Is there a pill I can take that will take all my pain away?' I told him that sadly, no, no such wondrous pill has been invented and likely never will. But I was wrong: this book is exactly that 'pill.' Dr. Lerner expertly and gently provides an easy-to-understand-and-apply prescription for restored health, hope and joy via the principle of resilience. If I could go back in time, I would place this book in my patient's hands and say, "Here it is! Here's your pill!"

~ David Anderson, Ph.D., Licensed Psychologist
Former Executive Director, Sierra Tucson and The Meadows

"What an important and timely book about thriving in today's crazy times. Jerome Lerner is the perfect person to write about building resilience. With his years of clinical work about resilience, and his own experiences with unimaginable loss, Jerry knows firsthand what it takes to build resilience as a habit and discipline in one's life. In this book, his elegant four-part model that shows you exactly how to be resilient. The work in this book should be required reading for everyone—from those embarking on the first stages of their careers and life, to seasoned leaders. It's a quick read with the potential for life-changing impact."

~ Andrew Neitlich, Author, Coach
Founder and Director of the Center for Executive Coaching

"In Unraveled to Unrivaled, Dr. Lerner gives us a hopeful message about the power and possibility of building resilience to recover from the adversity many people experience in life. Eloquently addressing biology, emotion, thought and interpersonal connections, Dr. Lerner speaks not just of treating disease, but of addressing the whole person in the thoughtful, compassionate way he has done his whole career. This is essential reading not just for medical providers, but for everyone."

~ Michael Genovese MD, JD
Chief Medical Officer, Acadia Healthcare

"I have had the pleasure to work with Dr. Lerner for over a decade, and his ongoing work around pain management and resiliency has impacted so many patients and their care and brings life-changing recovery. This book continues to build on his work and helps to shine a light on so many important factors that make a big difference in unraveling pain and trauma to build strong resiliency and resolve for patient care and treatment. I have personally applied many of these concepts and methodologies in my own work with patients as well as my personal self-care. I am privileged and honored to highly recommend this book and all the concepts and principles Dr. Lerner presents."

~ Michael L Gaziano LCSW
Executive Clinical Director, Recovery Ways

TABLE OF CONTENTS

ACKNOWLEDGMENTS / page xi

FOREWORD / page xiii
    by Jaime Welsh Vinck, MC, LPC

PREFACE / page xvii
    From Pain to Healing:
    Discovering the Four Dimensions of Resilience

INTRODUCTION / page 1
    Understanding Resilience

PART ONE:
    The Problem of Lost Resilience

    CHAPTER 1 / page 9
    Slings and Arrows

    CHAPTER 2 / page 17
    Sabre-toothed Tigers in the Twenty-first Century

    CHAPTER 3 / page 25
    First, We Make Our Choices

    CHAPTER 4 / page 39
    The Secrets to Sustainable Resilience

x

PART TWO:
Embracing the Four Dimensions of Resilience

CHAPTER 5 / page 47
The First Dimension of Resilience:
Resilient Biology

CHAPTER 6 / page 63
The Second of Dimension of Resilience:
Resilient Emotional Tone

CHAPTER 7 / page 75
The Third Dimension of Resilience:
Resilient Thinking

CHAPTER 8 / page 89
The Fourth Dimension of Resilience:
Resilient Connections

CHAPTER 9 / page 99
Working The "Four Tumblers"

TAKE A MOMENT ACTIVITIES / page 105

GLOSSARY / page 139

REFERENCES / page 143

ABOUT DR. LERNER / page 147

ACKNOWLEDGMENTS

This book would not have been written if not for the efforts and diligence of Gina Kilker. She has served as writing coach, listener, sounding board, note taker, idea challenger, organizer, editor and more. Gina, thank you from the bottom of my heart. Sincere thanks also to Chellie Buzzeo for her design work and Amy Rusk for editing.

I send my deep love and gratitude to my head cheerleader and unwavering supporter, my lovely always-bride, Stephanie Sikes. "Love you more!" Thanks to the circle of men who have unfailingly kept me grounded, focused, in touch and connected—Mitch, Don, Dave, Pat, Jeff, George, Rick and Dan. My thanks to the treatment programs and especially their caregivers who dedicate themselves to helping the most unraveled among us. I have had the privilege of working with and learning from two of the finest facilities—Sierra Tucson and The Meadows. Thanks as well to The Mankind Project for initiating me into a life of purpose, self-exploration, and connection.

I've had some ups, had some downs

Shared some laughs, been on the ground

And I'm still not all that I want to be

But I'm feeling alright now

Alright now

I still can't fly but I can walk

I'll get me there somehow

And I'm feeling alright now

"Alright Now"

Music and lyrics by Jerry Lerner

Available on LernerForLife.com

Listen to it now:

FOREWORD

by Jaime Welsh Vinck, MC, LPC

Years ago, while working in a residential treatment center, I had the honor of being a therapist for a brilliant, renowned singer. One day, while sharing his incredible wisdom he explained to me that in life there are two types of folks: those who are the Singers and those who are the Songs. When asked to elaborate, he explained that Singers are meant to be performing in front of a crowd; they carry the tune and bring music and lyrics to life to tell a story. Songs, on the other hand, love to hear others give voice to their creations as they provide musical notes, the syncopation, and the poetry that becomes the lyrics. Voila! The world finally made sense to me. For years I neatly organized my world into two categories: the Singers and the Songs, balancing each equally when forming teams, hosting parties, and even within my own family (in case you didn't guess, per my former client, I am a Song). This simple way of looking at the world was thrown out the window the day I met my colleague and friend, Dr. Jerry Lerner.

Dr. Lerner possesses the unique ability to be both the singer and the song. I know this to be true as I heard him play and sing a song that he had written to his lovely bride, Stephanie. I was so moved by his ability to be both singer and song, I asked him to perform at an important event opening, honoring a new behavioral health program. This program would expand our ability to help a highly acute population who were often marginalized and overlooked. Dr. Lerner agreed and performed "All Right Now," an original work that shared his resilience during the darkest days of his life,

both personally and professionally. His song instilled hope and provided inspirations. More importantly, his story came to life in his own voice, to his own melody.

Dr. Lerner's book, "Unraveled to Unrivaled, Embracing the Four Dimension of Resilience," is a practical guide to building our strength in a holistic manner, mind, body, and spirit. His acknowledgment that we are multi-faceted beings, and that healing isn't always linear, speaks to his deep understanding of the human psyche. He weaves inspirational stories into each section, and with great humility speaks of his patient's growth, hope, and letting go of their pain. When we worked together from a clinical perspective; I witnessed his gifts moving through the lives of others. Dr. Lerner's mindfulness workshops and pain coaching were important components to patients' hope and healing, as well as to our staff's growth. Patient care was always top of mind, and in one of our first experiences working together, he advocated mightily for his patients who suffered from chronic pain to have warm bath robes when they got out of their hydrotherapy. Together we made this happen, and the patients were incredibly grateful for this seemingly small thing that provided them comfort and dignity — mind, body, and spirit. As Medical Director, Dr. Lerner was a tireless advocate for patient safety and reasonable caseloads for therapists and medical providers, as well as appropriate staffing ratios for nurses. No detail was too small for his interest: and no issue was too large for him to boldly tackle.

As an inspirational speaker, Dr. Lerner also touched many audiences filled with clinicians, physicians, and folks outside of our field (mature adults) by sharing his knowledge and experience, providing hope that they, too, could build their own resilience. One large audience in Los Angeles was even treated to the information that Dr. Lerner had in fact played Tevye, the lead in the musical Fiddler on the Roof, infusing levity to an otherwise overwhelmingly emotional topic.

I have also witnessed Dr. Lerner lose his trust in an organization's leadership and become disillusioned, as many of us have at times. We did not work together for a while, and when I became a CEO, one of my top goals was to convince Dr. Lerner to return. The road was not easy, trust had to be re-established as he wasn't ready, and it also required a professional pivot. Dr. Lerner's return to our team required additional training, testing, and a shift to primary addiction work when I asked him to take over the Impaired Professionals Program. Working on behalf of impaired professionals Dr. Lerner undertook this challenge with his customary grace, demonstrating a humility that I don't often see in accomplished and seasoned professionals (especially physicians). We worked together for a few more years and Dr. Lerner provided hope and healing to countless physicians and nurses, who had everything to lose and no idea how to change.

Even prior to COVID-19, our nation was in the midst of a suicide epidemic and opioid crisis. This has been exacerbated since the pandemic, with alcohol abuse becoming more prevalent and lethal than it ever has been. Our lives have all been touched by grief, loss, and trauma. As both leaders and clinicians in the treatment industry, I know that we are working tirelessly to expand access to ethical quality care and to establish the behavioral health industry as one of science, evidence, and credibility. I am grateful to have stood in the fire of our time, shoulder-to-shoulder with Dr. Lerner, and I'm honored to have been asked to write the foreword for his book. "Unraveled to Unrivaled" is perfectly timed and essential reading for all who want to learn to harness our strength and resilience so that we are thriving, not just surviving, in our one precious life.

Jaime Welsh Vinck MC, LPC
Chief Executive Officer
CPF Recovery Ways

PREFACE
From Pain to Healing: Discovering the Four Dimensions of Resilience

The seeds of this book started in the 1980s. At that time, I was medical director of a rehabilitation hospital focused on major disabling conditions, such as stroke, head injuries, spinal cord injuries, amputations, etc. It was in that setting that I saw a great number of people struggling with physical and emotional pain. I noticed that many people got better and responded to good care and treatment, but there were others who did not do so well. They received the same good treatment for the same conditions, and yet their pain and suffering persisted. I decided that it was time to open a pain clinic, and, along with some very talented and expert colleagues, did just that. But this wasn't going to be just any pain clinic. We were going to work with the people who did not respond well to conventional treatment. The challenge for all of us was to figure out what was keeping them stuck, and what was holding them back from responding and healing with proven care and treatment. The world was labeling these people with "chronic

pain." My colleagues and I preferred to call it "complicated pain." We chose to call it "complicated" rather than "chronic" pain to indicate that it means multiple factors, intertwined and difficult to understand; and it could improve when these complicating factors were addressed.

On the physical side of things, we incorporated several cutting-edge approaches that at the time were not accepted into the mainstream. Nowadays these are very familiar and accepted modalities, including myofascial release and acupuncture. On the psychological side, we became aware that many people with unresolved pain were showing signs and symptoms very similar to post-traumatic stress disorder (PTSD). At that time PTSD was something medicine thought of as more related to soldiers at war or people who had sustained life-threatening events, such as rape or assault. Our patients rarely reported their PTSD-like symptoms unless we asked about them because they were so focused on the physical pain and suffering and the need for relief. So, in addition to our physical treatment of pain we began exploring therapies that would help people work through the psychologically traumatic events related to their painful conditions—most commonly work injuries or serious car collisions. Working through these traumas in a therapeutic manner opened the door for physical healing in a surprising and reproducible way.

However, by opening the door to explore trauma, we began to discover that most people we worked with were holding other unresolved traumatic events unrelated to their physical pain that needed to be addressed in order for healing to proceed.

The treatment of trauma, PTSD, and healing of adverse childhood experiences are currently in the forefront of modern psychology and therapy. But in 1991, when we opened our pain clinic, this field was in its infancy. One of the therapies frequently used today for trauma, EMDR, was barely on the radar in the field of psychology and trauma and was considered unproven—if not quackery. Another current approach to treating trauma is Somatic Experiencing. The first book referring to this technique ("Waking the Tiger," Peter Levine) was published five years after our clinic opened. We relied instead on techniques called SomatoEmotional Release and myofascial unwinding. I went through training in both of these approaches so that I could not only prescribe and recommend these therapies, but also participate in them. We saw some marvelous results and breakthroughs utilizing the combination of our innovative physical techniques and working through unresolved trauma. But that's not the end of the story. The mid-1990s into the 2000s experienced an explosion of medical specialists in the field of pain management. This was driven at least in part by an expansion of what is called interventional pain management—the treatment of pain through injections and other minimally invasive procedures (epidurals, facet blocks, implants, etc.) and through an ever-increasing reliance on opioid pain medications. I believe this drove the field of pain management away from acknowledging and treating the traumatic and emotional aspects of pain. It also contributed greatly to an opiate epidemic.

Opiate abuse and addiction became a more and more common aspect of pain management, requiring more vigorous assessment, observation, and testing to attempt to stay on top of it. I was becoming restless to practice one way, while the field was heading another way. I longed to find a way to practice where pain, trauma, mood, and addiction could all be cared for in an integrative and holistic manner.

The year 2008 changed my life. My son, Gabriel was senselessly murdered, and I found myself with the worst emotional pain imaginable. My grief has been nearly unbearable at times and it continues to require every resilience strategy I can muster in order to stay on a healthy and positive path.

Part of my healing was to find work that was meaningful and fulfilling. In 2010 I came across a job posting—medical director of a pain program at a world-famous facility in Tucson, Arizona, offering residential integrative treatment for addictions, trauma, mood, and pain. Within a few months I had moved halfway across the country to start a new journey. Here I saw and cared for people with every combination of pain, trauma, depression, anxiety, and grief. With every sort of treatment and therapy I could have dreamed of being available, I could truly observe the possibilities of healing. While working there I also studied and became board certified in addiction medicine.

Eventually, I was able to shape the program into what we called Complicated Pain Recovery. I lectured to patients there regularly and developed a series of presentations that first held the basic conceptual components of the Four Dimensions of Resilience. I began to lecture to professionals nationally with a message that there are really four aspects of chronic pain, only one of which is physical. The lectures were so well received that I developed a two-day workshop to train behavioral health and addiction specialists, which I enjoyed greatly. The feedback I got repeatedly is that my conceptual model applied to all patients, not only those with chronic pain. Therapists and counselors were using it with their clients and were changed in their own personal lives based on the ideas in my model.

There was a real need and longing to grasp and apply the principles of resilience. Over time my clinical work moved away from pain management and into working with addictions with co-occurring mood and trauma challenges. My lecture materials evolved into a series I called Resilience Recovery, which I presented weekly to patients. Over and over after my lectures, patients came up and asked if I had a book with this material. Eureka! I began to see that there was a real need and longing to grasp and apply the principles of resilience. The creation of the Resilience Recovery model and this book, "Unraveled to Unrivaled: Embracing the Four Dimensions of Resilience," is the product of three decades as a Physician, continually asking, "Why do some people respond well to good care while others remain stuck?" I believe the answer is loss of resilience. This book is my effort to explain the problem of lost resilience, how to reclaim it, and most importantly, how to sustain resilience over a lifetime.

Jerry Lerner MD
Executive Coach
LERNER For Life

INTRODUCTION
Understanding Resilience

This is a book about resilience, what it is, how we lose it, and how we reclaim it. Resilience is a fancy word for living your best life in all ways possible—resilient biology, resilient emotional tone, resilient thinking, and resilient interconnections.

The Japanese have a proverb, "Nana korobi, ya oki" that roughly translates to "fall down seven times, get up eight."

Nat King Cole sang about it beautifully in **Pick Yourself Up:** "Nothing's impossible I have found/for when my chin is on the ground/I pick myself up/dust myself off/start all over again."[i]

Life has its ups and downs. Sometimes it's like the gentle waves of a peaceful lake. Other times it feels like a Tsunami. On a daily basis we navigate these ups and downs. When things are tough, what choice do we have but to pick ourselves up, dust ourselves off, and start all over again? Yet, there are times in everyone's life when getting up and moving forward seems daunting. Resilience is what keeps us going. The American Psychological Association defines resilience as "the process and outcome of successfully adapting to difficult or challenging life experiences, especially through

mental, emotional, and behavioral flexibility and adjustment to external and internal demands."

> *Resilience is synonymous with life.*
> *All life is born soft and supple.*
> *In death all becomes stiff and hard.*
> *The hard and stiff will become broken.*
> *The soft and supple will prevail.* [ii]
>
> ~ Adapted from Steven Mitchell's translation of Tao Te Ching

If resilience has the qualities of energy—flexibility and forward motion, loss of resilience is more like inertia; an object at rest stays at rest, and an object in motion stays in motion unless acted upon by an outside force. With loss of resilience we feel stuck, an "object at rest," unable to find the energy to move forward. Or, our lives are heading in the wrong direction, as an "object in motion," careening in a negative trajectory, unable to make corrections. Applying the principles and strategies presented in the second section of this book creates that "outside force," which resolves inertia, restoring and sustaining resilience. Without the understanding, tools, and strategies required to maintain resilience, we find ourselves at risk of declining health, physical and emotional distress, and loss of hope and direction.

Emotional pain, tragedy and loss are unavoidable experiences in life. For me, my deepest despair was the murder of my son, Gabriel. Gabe had an amazing future ahead of him. He had graduated college with honors, completed law school at a prestigious university, and had just obtained a position as law clerk to a wonderful federal judge. One Sunday he was on his way to do volunteer work with youth and kindly stopped on a rural road to give two strangers a ride. They assaulted him and then shot him. As I write this, 14 years have passed. The loss will always impact me.

Having resilience does not mean it will be easy nor that it will erase all of our suffering. Sometimes it just means getting through the days until we find ourselves again. I have experienced much emotional pain and, yet, I have created a life that is generally happy and healthy enough to hold the loss and the love for my son. There are no secrets here. My survival requires me to utilize every resilience tool in my toolbox. Ongoing and repeatedly, early on and still, it is the support of friends and family who show compassion and caring around my waves of intense emotions. It is finding my way through a grieving process that, even though it has improved, never goes away. For me, it is about having a sense of meaning and purpose in the world while maintaining a sense of humor. It also requires a heightened level of self-care, managing stress levels, exercising regularly, and just taking time to listen to my needs.

I have come to understand that resilience isn't some fluffy New Age, self-help slogan. It is work and can be messy, but even in the hardest of times, it is the work we are called to do; and it is the only way through to the other side. My own efforts to survive and thrive through my loss are woven into the fabric of this book, as is the spirit of my son, Gabriel.

One way to conceptualize resilience is to look at it as a continuum. At best our lives move between a state of harmony (peaceful, happy, content) and disharmony (stressed, challenged, discontent).

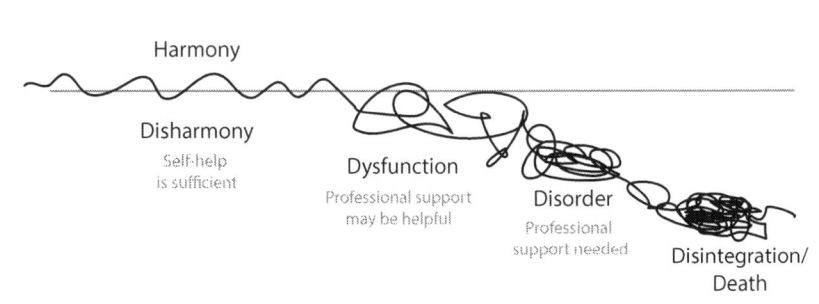

The Resilience Continuum illustrates how our moods and our responses to our moods fluctuate from day to day. Our resilience is challenged when it is difficult to move from a state of disharmony back to a state of harmony. Without a strong base of resilience, we can disintegrate and spiral toward a more serious state.

Dysfunction can present in myriad ways, such as decreased energy and enthusiasm, overuse of alcohol or other addictive substances, or simply loss of joy and pleasure with life. Dysfunctional living, when unaddressed, spirals downward to a chaotic disordered state, a more perilous form of inertia. This can include psychological disorders, such as depression and generalized anxiety—or physical disorders, such as cardiovascular disease and diabetes.

Disorders related to loss of resilience, if not effectively cared for, lead to a breakdown of the system. This manifests as degenerative conditions, such as premature aging, serious physical and psychological breakdown, and even death.

Embracing the Four Dimensions of Resilience (4DRs) is the process of reversing the downward spiral—whether from the unavoidable moments of disharmony or the longer journey of recovery from disorders back to restored well-being. Wherever you are in the resilience continuum, the correct time to invest in resilience is now. Like a savings account, the longer we make regular "deposits" the more we have available when needed.

The word resilience appears often in this book. Perhaps it would be more accurate to say "resiliences." I have come to understand through my education, personal experience, and three decades of working with patients and clients, that there are multiple dimensions of resilience that, when synergized, maximize health and well-being. It would be even more accurate to make the word into a verb, "resiliencing," since, as you will discover in this book, creating and sustaining resilience is an active, ongoing process.

If you Google the word resilience you will discover an abundance of books and articles on the subject. These can all be helpful in their own right; however, most address only one or perhaps two of the aspects of resilience. They imply by omission that they are discussing the totality of resilience. For example, some writings will talk about resilience as a psychological quality, while others focus on resilience biologically; and yet others suggest that having meaning and purpose is the driving force behind resilience.

This book proposes that there are Four Dimensions of Resilience. These dimensions are distinct, yet entirely interwoven. It was only through working through the difficulties of my own life, my involvement with hundreds of patients and clients who trusted me with their lives and struggles, and the incessant question in my head—why do some people recover from their adversities and others don't?—that I was able to puzzle this together.

The Four Dimensions

DR1	DR2	DR3	DR4
Resilient Biology	Resilient Emotional Tone	Resilient Thinking	Resilient Connections
The lifestyle choices and habits needed for optimal health and energy.	The capacity to minimize time in survival mode and maximize time being present and creative.	The ability to think compassionately towards ourselves and to focus on positive goals.	Connecting with ourselves, connecting with others in positive, supportive relationships, and connecting to the world through meaning, purpose or passion.

In the following four chapters we will explore the loss of resilience in greater depth. We will see how and why many of us disconnect from the cycle of harmony/disharmony, spiraling downward to states of dysfunction and disorder. In part two of the book, I will lay out all the strategies and tools that give us the capacity to reverse that cycle and sustain a resilient life.

PART ONE:
The Problem of Lost Resilience

CHAPTER 1
Slings and Arrows

*"Whether it is nobler in the mind to suffer
The slings and arrows of outrageous fortune,
Or to take arms against a sea of troubles
And by opposing end them."*
~ Hamlet, William Shakespeare, English playwright and poet

"Until you make the unconscious conscious, it will direct your life and you will call it fate." [iii]
~ Carl Jung, Swiss psychiatrist and psychoanalyst

The slings and arrows of life are unavoidable. They are the disharmonies of the harmony/disharmony continuum. Hamlet ponders ending it all to escape his sufferings—**To be or not to be**—only to question if even in death he might still dream, continuing to experience the pain he is trying to escape in life.

How we respond to our own slings and arrows greatly determines the direction of our lives. As we face them, feel and accept the pain, and make peace with them, we grow and heal. Often, however, we are tempted to avoid our suffering as Hamlet was. We do so with distractions or with attempts to numb or deny our emotions. These strategies are never successful. Whatever suffering we suppress or numb in our conscious lives shouts out in our subconscious. Our pain will be heard, one way or another. If not faced and accepted directly it becomes our "fate," as Jung aptly puts it. It surfaces as anxiety, depression, addiction, relationship dysfunction or physical ailments. Hamlet at some level intuits this truth—that attempts to escape life's woes are impossible. "To sleep, perchance to dream—ay, there's the rub."

The unaddressed and unresolved slings and arrows of life are a major part of what leads to loss of resilience. An accumulation of adverse events, especially in our developing years, can be particularly harmful to our well-being. So, let's start at the beginning—our childhood experiences and their impact on resilience.

Adverse Childhood Experiences

Kaiser Permanente, one of the largest nonprofit healthcare plans in the United States, conducted extensive studies in the mid-1990s focusing on the effect of adverse childhood experiences. The Adverse Childhood Experience (ACEs) research studied 1700 people for the impact that adverse childhood events had in adulthood. These include physical or verbal abuse, physical or emotional neglect, experiencing parental separation or divorce, as well as alcoholism or addiction in the household. Also included is the child observing the abuse of another family member and/or the presence of mental illness and suicide within the home. The data clearly shows that the more adverse experiences one has in childhood, the higher the risk is in adulthood for developing a long list of health problems and associated poor quality of life —problems as diverse as alcohol abuse/addiction, depression, illicit drug use, obesity, chronic obstructive pulmonary disease, ischemic heart disease and even fetal death!

How can bad things happening in our childhoods negatively affect our mental and physical health so severely, for the rest of our lives? The common denominator is the experience of repeatedly feeling unsafe or unseen. Both the presence of repeated hurts and the absence of adequate love and attention from family members is enough to literally change our biology during developmental years. Repeated adverse events impact the resilience continuum until the child lives in a perpetual dysfunctional state. This is known as "survival mode" in trauma literature, where we move between states of fight, flight, or freeze, (anger, fear or shutting down—more about that in the next chapter). This state of dysfunctional existence is certainly not the fault of the child. It is, in fact, mostly invisible to the child, like a fish in water or a mammal breathing air. Also, many of these events occur before we have the language or conceptual framework to understand and process them. Later in life we may look back and come to recognize what happened. This cognitive understanding, however, does not equate to normalizing our nervous systems. These slings and arrows come to reside within our very cells and tissues. This is how, over many years, we become more prone to the whole spectrum of mental illness and degenerative medical conditions.

Lest this sound hopeless, it is very possible to reverse and ameliorate these risks and outcomes. I have been privileged to meet and work with many who have. Doing the work of diligently addressing the Four Dimensions of Resilience (4DRs) goes a long way in recovering our well-being. There are effective strategies to heal the wounds we carry and support our nervous system through any residual impact of past adversities. Thus, the quote by Jung at the beginning of this chapter: "Until you make the unconscious conscious, it will direct your life and you will call it fate." The mostly unconscious impact of our personal slings and arrows become our fate—mentally, emotionally and physically—until brought to light and healed.

A note of caution here. Recovering our well-being is not the same as curing us from the effects of these ACEs. We may be able to cure pneumonia with a course of antibiotics. But restoring and maintaining resilience is an ongoing and lifelong commitment to recovery. Like exercise, we don't get in shape by working out once. Physical fitness calls for regular, ongoing effort. Even after years of conditioning, all the health benefits begin to disappear as soon as the regular exercise ends. Likewise, engaging the principles and strategies of the 4DRs is a lifetime commitment.

Curious about your own ACEs score? Visit cdc.gov/violence prevention/aces/about.html. Another measurement that can be taken is the Health Resiliency Stress Questionnaire (HRSQ). Originally designed for primary care and mental health providers, it can be self-administered. It takes just a few minutes to complete and provides a quick overview of a person's ability to tolerate and cope with stress in relation to one's health. Like the ACEs assessment, the questionnaire connects the identification of personal strengths and perceptions to early life adversity. The HRSQ is free and can be found here: pacesconnection.com.

Acute Trauma

While ACEs create a major challenge to strong resilience, there are other factors that create the same fight/flight/freeze over-activity. Acute traumatic events often activate this survival response. When severe and persistent, we call it Post-Traumatic Stress Disorder, or PTSD. These events include civilians and soldiers in war zones, assault, abuse, neglect, and near fatal car accidents; the list goes on and on. Any distressing or threatening event that exceeds our capacity to cope may evoke PTSD, depending on our resilience strengths, support systems, and unhealed ACEs.

Also negatively impacting resilience is trans-generational trauma. Studies show that unresolved trauma can be passed from generation to generation. I observed this directly with my Jewish parents and adult relatives who continued to embody and express the trauma that was directly experienced by my grandparents' Holocaust generation. The traumas of slavery oppression, and prejudice continue to reverberate throughout the generations of our society, affecting us all in adverse ways, often unconsciously.

Grief and Loss

Grief plays a major role in losing resilience. Loss of a loved one, expected or unexpected, may drain us of the energy to maintain healthy habits and do meaningful activities that are necessary for resilience. Isolation and withdrawal from social activity further impede resilience. Certainly, grief needs to be honored and experienced. However, maintaining resilience strategies even through this time of loss is necessary for coming through the experience whole on the other side. Grief is not only about losing people. Loss of a job, marriage or relationship, a family pet, or security and health all deserve a mourning period. Practicing resilience during these times can eliminate any unnecessary and prolonged suffering.

Prolonged Stress

As stated previously, we all go through cycles of harmony and disharmony in life. Sometimes though, stresses remain too persistent or intense to bounce back. Prolonged stress and conflict at work or at home create a sustained disharmony that will turn into dysfunction if not addressed. Add to this list financial woes, job loss or insecurity, ill health in ourselves or those we care about. Embracing the 4DRs enhances our capacity to tolerate stress, calm ourselves, visualize change and take needed action.

TAKE A MOMENT ACTIVITY
Know Your Level of Resilience

Following is an informal self-assessment to help you gain insight into your current state of resilience.

Rate each of the following statements ranging from 1 to 5.

1	2	3	4	5
You totally disagree				You strongly agree

_____ I tend to bounce back quickly after stressful times.

_____ When I get upset, I generally calm down quickly.

_____ I am generally hopeful about life.

_____ I feel loved and supported.

_____ I ask for help when I need it.

_____ I have healthy and trusting relationships.

_____ My overall physical health is good.

_____ I choose healthy activities to decrease stress.

_____ I exercise at least 3 times per week.

_____ I generally feel well rested.

_____ My diet is generally healthy.

_____ I am compassionate toward myself.

_____ **TOTAL**

SCORING

>30	30-39	40-49	50-60
High resilience risk	Moderate resilience risk	Resilient	Very resilient

The impact of the many slings and arrows of life, whether from childhood experiences, adult tragedies, stressful life conditions or generational atrocities, greatly impacts our resilience. Unrecognized and unresolved trauma continues to impact us neurobiologically, influencing long-term physical, mental and biological health. Identifying and resolving the emotional impact of trauma has a profound effect on well-being. Learning the principles and practices of the 4DRs provides a path to recovering and sustaining resilience. In the following chapter we will take a deeper dive into how living in survival mode compromises resilience.

CHAPTER 2
Sabre-toothed Tigers in the Twenty-first Century

"It's not stress that kills us, it's our reaction to it." [iv]
~ Hans Selye, Austro-Hungarian scientist

"Imagine a land where people are afraid of dragons. It is a reasonable fear: dragons possess a number of qualities that make being afraid of them a very commendable response. Things like their terrible size, their ability to spout fire and to crack boulders into splinters with their massive talons. In fact, the only terrifying quality that dragons do not possess is that of existence." [v]
~ David Whiteland, American author

Imagine one of our ancient human ancestors foraging for food. Suddenly a quiet rustling noise is noticed. A quick turn of the head, and there is a Sabre-toothed tiger fast approaching! Quicker than thought, with the lightning speed and intensity of instinct, our ancestor is taking action. If possible, a mad dash for the cave.

If not, climb the nearest tree. Nowhere to flee? Turn and fight. Grab a stick or a stone. Do whatever it takes to survive.

Without this amazing and powerful instinctual response, we would not be here today. You and I, much like our ancestors and every human being and animal on earth, have built within us an instinct to survive when mortally threatened. This instinct is called "fight or flight" because those are the two options available for each of us to survive any life-threatening situation. While this survival response is normal and necessary in a life-threatening situation, it is problematic if activated when no imminent danger is truly present. Fight/flight is the primary function of the survival nervous system. When activated, adrenaline is released, coursing through our blood. Our heart races, blood pressure rises—all to make us as fast and as strong as possible to oppose the threat before us. These biological reactions have a rightful place when they help us to escape danger. But when we are stuck in traffic, worried about our job, or in conflict with a loved one, why do we biologically react as if we are about to be attacked by a wild animal?

Although we live in a world where physical threats are relatively rare compared to our distant ancestors, we retain the same instinctual responses they relied upon to survive And because of our amazing human brains, we imagine possible threats that are not present, anticipate future events that may or may not happen or remember events from our past that are distressful. Our bodies respond to these internal images as though they are real and present dangers.

Living in survival mode when not faced by an immediate threat decreases our ability to be resilient in handling life's challenges. Our brain and biology are primed for running or fighting, as though there is a need to escape an approaching disaster rather than handling the embarrassment of a fumbled business presentation. Why? Because when we encounter something that seems abstractly threatening, like a presentation gone bad, our brains look for what dangers may lie within the situation. In the flash of a second, often wordlessly and subconsciously, the mind goes from the idea that a bad presentation means my job is at risk, to the thought that if I lose my job I won't be able to pay the rent; and then, how will I live and eat and take care of myself and my family? The endpoint of this disaster cascade feels like a survival risk, and we react with the same biology as an immediate threat. Our imagination has sent images and messages to the ancient survival center of the brain where threats are identified. The brain revs up the survival nervous system, activating fight or flight mode. Depending on experience and our skill in practicing self-regulation, our sympathetic response may be scaled to the degree of actual threat, triggering intense anxiety or even a panic attack —all because a presentation went awry.

The Biology of Survival

To understand survival response requires a brief lesson in biology. The fight/flight system we have been discussing resides within the central nervous system (CNS). The CNS consists of the brain and spinal cord. The CNS can be further divided into the voluntary and autonomic nervous system. The voluntary part of the system is just what it sounds like. These are the conscious choices and actions we take, such as me typing the words on this page. When we choose what to eat and what clothes to wear, we are operating through this voluntary nervous system.

The other part of the CNS, the autonomic nervous system, consists of all the automatic functions that happen behind the scenes, typically without conscious awareness. Body temperature, heart rate, digestion, immune response to bacteria and viruses—these and thousands of other functions are happening outside our awareness 24/7. If we had to consciously monitor and manage these operations, we would have no time to work, play or sleep.

The autonomic system is further divided into the parasympathetic and sympathetic nervous system (PNS and SNS). The PNS regulates the day-to-day, automatic functions of living. It is often called the "rest and digest" system, regulating everything from food processing to getting sleepy at night. It is also involved in our capacity to socialize, and to read and understand facial expressions. The SNS, on the other hand, assures survival. It detects threats and activates the instinctual response to survive—to fight or run from danger. When activated, it elicits a powerful surge of energy, all focused on survival. In moments of threat, energy is diverted from the PNS functions of digestion, immunity, sleep, and socializing. After all, what good is digesting breakfast if you're about to become lunch for an approaching tiger?

In addition to fight and flight, there is also a third survival response called "freeze." Unlike the powerful energizing effect of SNS activation, freeze is connected to an old part of the PNS. It has the effect of shutting everything down. This response may occur when neither running or fighting is an option. It is most likely an evolutionary response to discourage being eaten or harmed ("playing possum"), or it may lessen pain in the face of imminent death. In humans it may appear as disassociation, which is mentally and emotionally disappearing from a stressful or threatening situation.

No One to Fight and Nowhere to Run

We humans are all stuck with this instinctual system, along with our animal counterparts. The difference between other animals and humans is that animals, for the most part, only activate the SNS in true life-threatening situations, while we humans activate our survival response for all manner of perceived threats—imagined, remembered, or theoretical. I like to call these "metaphorical threats." Also, our animal friends shake off their fight/flight response immediately after it is no longer helpful, sometimes literally shivering to release tension and excess adrenaline. They then return efficiently to a balanced way of functioning, bringing back online the parasympathetic system. To humans' detriment, we can hang onto our survival responses long after there is a hint of a real threat, sometimes for hours, days, or even years. We do this by remembering, replaying or rehearsing for the next time something bad happens.

My dog Lili never worries about paying the rent. She isn't stressed about running out of food. She is blessed with the incapacity to abstract thoughts into worry. Conversely, we humans are experts at creating stress by merely thinking. We take metaphorical threats such as, "My job may be at risk," and subconsciously chase it down the rabbit hole to "I won't be able to pay the rent, etc." Our fight/flight becomes activated, a biological response identical to our ancestor's reaction to seeing the Sabre-toothed tiger. Rather than calling it fight/flight/freeze, we are more familiar with the terms worry, upset, anxiety or stress. But it is the same thing. This type of survival response to metaphorical threats is one of the great struggles of modern humanity. Career worries, relationship conflicts, traffic jams, unexpected bills, watching the evening news—these all activate the body's sympathetic nervous system. But for these types of metaphorical threats there is no one to fight and nowhere to run! Even so, adrenaline surges, muscles tense in preparation to fight or we move restlessly with the urge to flee.

As though this is not enough of a challenge for all of us, consider the compounding complication of shouldering adverse childhood experiences (ACEs) or unresolved adult trauma, as was discussed in the previous chapter. These factors hypersensitize the survival nervous system, making it likely we will respond more intensely and for longer duration to stressful events and "metaphorical threats."

Consider a former client of mine, Tod, and his friend Ted. Tod was walking in the park with Ted after a game of frisbee. While they were strolling and enjoying the blue sky and green foliage, an off-leash golden retriever came running in hot pursuit of a tennis ball. The retriever spotted Ted, frisbee in hand, and changed course in hopes of playing. Ted laughed at the sight of the happy dog. Tod, on the other hand, stepped immediately behind Ted, fearing an attack from the dog. Tod's reaction to this non-threatening situation was a result of being bitten by a dog during childhood. He was hypersensitized by a childhood trauma.

Tina was a patient I worked with regarding a different kind of trauma. She was hanging out with a group of friends one day when one of them came up from behind her and placed a hand on her shoulder in a gesture of friendship. Tina cringed and tensed from the unexpected touch: her survival response was triggered by an assault that had occurred years before. Tina came into treatment to heal the effects of that trauma and learn how to reclaim a calmer nervous system.

The Problem of Sabre-toothed Tigers in the 21st Century

Living in a prolonged state of high alert and stress when there is no one to fight and nothing to run from is detrimental to our physical and mental health. During the survival response our bodies divert all energy to prepare for fight or flight. Anything that is not required for immediate survival is placed on the back burner. This means that parasympathetic functions like digestion, immune response and tissue repair are all temporarily impaired or halted. The temporary reduction in parasympathetic function is not a problem when it occurs briefly to escape a real-life predator or life-threatening event. However, when our bodies are in constant survival mode reacting to the metaphorical threats around us, we become exhausted. Unneeded muscle tension results in headaches and back pain; impaired gastrointestinal activity leads to upset stomach and indigestion; sleep is disrupted, and immune response is weakened, making us more vulnerable to any cold, flu, or virus going around.

Making matters worse, the survival SNS resides primarily in the more primitive, instinctual part of the brain. When activated it inhibits access to the areas of the brain involved with creativity, higher thinking and problem solving, the very tools needed to battle 21st century Sabre-toothed tigers. This is where the resilience strategies come in. We can become more proficient at remaining calm, present, and focused. We are capable of more efficiently returning from a state of disharmony to a place of harmony after we've been triggered.

Not All Stress Is Bad

I don't want to end this subject without pointing out that not all sympathetic activation is bad. Consciously chosen, it can be a source of enjoyment and pleasure. It can help us to grow physically, emotionally and psychologically. It can help us complete important goals. Take exercise for example. Working out is a form of physical stress. Done appropriately and at reasonable intervals, this type of stress improves strength and cardiovascular capacity, and lowers systemic inflammation (more about that in the next chapter). It is also a great reliever of dis-stress. Another example of activation is learning, a form of cognitive or mental stress. Preparing for a final exam, learning to play an instrument, or mastering a new language can lead to growth and great satisfaction. Purposeful stress can even be fun, whether riding a rollercoaster, cheering for your favorite sports team, watching an action movie or performing for an audience. In the ever-shifting continuum of harmony/disharmony, these voluntary forms of sympathetic activation fall on the side of enhancing harmony. They make for some of the best moments of our lives.

TAKE A MOMENT ACTIVITY
Are You in Survival Mode?

Survival mode involves three core emotions: anger (fight), fear (flight) and numbness (freeze). Take a look at the words below that are associated with those core emotions How often are you experiencing these states? If your answer is rarely or occasionally, you are doing well. If your answer is often or most of the time, you are probably living predominantly in survival mode.

Core Emotion	Symptoms
Flight	Fear, anxious, worried, panicked, frightened, uneasy, apprehensive
Fight	Angry, annoyed, irritated, resentful, outraged, incensed, furious, impatient
Freeze	Numb, shut down, disconnected, empty

Learning and practicing resilience skills will help restore a more balanced life. Keep reading.

CHAPTER 3
First, We Make Our Choices

"Our lives are fashioned by our choices. First, we make our choices. Then our choices make us." [vi]

~ Anne Frank, German-Jewish author

"A habit cannot be tossed out the window; it must be coaxed down the stairs a step at a time." [vii]

~ Mark Twain, American author

The choices we make—consciously or unconsciously, thoughtfully or impulsively, creatively or in fear—eventually come to define our lives. Cumulatively, our choices make us who we are. These choices impact our ability to be resilient, especially during life's difficult moments. We often call repeated choices "habits" or even equate them with personality traits. Unconsciously repeated over and over again, our choices indeed become our fate. I contend that habits can be changed, and fate can be altered. We do this through practicing the 4DRs, the focus of part two of this book.

John was a patient of mine in a residential treatment program. At the time we met he had been using drugs for over 20 years. He told me that as a teen, his home life was miserable. His parents fought often, and the household was tense. He felt unseen, unsupported and sometimes scared and angry. Instead of spending time at home, he much preferred being around his new friends from high school. They introduced him to a world of alcohol and drugs. With these substances John could finally escape his deep-seated sadness and distress. It was easier to relax and have some fun. Starting with alcohol, then marijuana, his drug use escalated to cocaine and oxycodone, always striving to more effectively escape the pain inside and just have a good time. John's parents, distracted by their own marital problems, rarely noticed he was away with friends. They also didn't know he was developing a dangerous drug addiction.

As a teen, John could not articulate what I would call his "numbing strategies" to cope with an intolerable home life. He had no healthy role models and was offered no productive strategies to calm his anxieties. The "choice" he made to use drugs was unconscious. Nonetheless, this choice eventually "made him"—in this case into a drug addict. After twenty years, drugs had depleted John's resilience. He lacked the emotional maturation to identify and feel his emotions. His lifestyle lacked proper nutrition, exercise and sleep. He had spiraled from disharmony to dysfunction while in high school and soon thereafter was trapped by his disorder.

In treatment, John was forced to abstain from substances and for the first time came face to face with his underlying emotional pain from childhood, as well as the added shame of the life he came to live. His head became clear enough to recognize the origins of his behaviors; and, over time, he was able to forgive himself and his parents. Also, in the confines of treatment, John experienced for the first time the benefits of routine: eating three meals a day, going to sleep and waking up at regular hours, and getting daily physical activity. He met others who were dealing with similar struggles and experienced healthy, supportive relationships for the first time. I knew if John could turn these new behaviors into ongoing "choices," they would become healthy habits: and these in turn would change the course of his life for the better.

Eliminating habits that do us harm and replacing them with a lifestyle that enhances well-being, such as John did, is the path to restoring resilience. John's dysfunctional crutch was drugs. Whenever we lack robust resilience, there is some "choice" or habit that is problematic. Are we avoiding difficult emotions through improper use of food, alcohol, sex, gaming, or internet use? Are we neglecting our bodily needs through poor diet, a sedentary lifestyle or inadequate sleep? Are we immersed in self-blame and negative thoughts that only pull us down? Are we disconnected from healthy and supportive relationships? Have we lost a sense of direction or purpose?

Of course the stressors that lead us down an unhealthy path are not always due to difficulties growing up. Perhaps we have been on top of our game or at least doing fine, living a generally healthy and satisfying life when an unexpected event or major life change diverts our course. Job loss, health concerns, or the loss of a loved one can quickly derail a resilient lifestyle if we are not careful to sustain it. Even positive events—getting that dream job, the birth of a child, or winning the lottery—can result in disengaging from the choices and habits that have maintained our resilience.

It's time to take a deeper look at the choices and habits that determine a resilient life. We'll explore three major categories: Lifestyle choices, habits of thought, and healthy connections.

Lifestyle Choices

> *"Be careful about reading health books. You may die of a misprint."* [viii]
>
> ~ Mark Twain, American author

Lifestyle choices and habits go a long way in determining our resilience. The core components of lifestyle are diet, exercise, stress management, sleep, and avoidance of addictive toxins. Performing these poorly creates a biology that makes us prone to moodiness, impulsivity and depression. It causes unnecessary body aches and pain. Unhealthy lifestyle choices also accelerate aging and chronic diseases, such as cardiovascular disease, diabetes, arthritis and even dementia. The common denominator is something called systemic inflammation.

Systemic inflammation, also known as metabolic or chronic inflammation, should not be confused with acute inflammation. Acute inflammation is a normal, healthy and necessary response to injury and illness. The acute inflammatory response is the body's way of fighting infection and repairing damaged tissue and structures. It is called acute because it happens immediately following bodily harm. It is called inflammation because it literally heats things up. We have all experienced this—as redness and swelling after a bruise, scrape or cut. We know it as the fever that accompanies the flu or pneumonia. These are the outward signs of increased blood flow and the arrival of killer and scavenger cells to remove damaged tissue or kill infectious agents. We could not survive without this lifesaving acute response. Wounds would not heal and infections would overtake us.

This is a far cry from systemic, chronic inflammation. As the term implies, it is widespread throughout the body, rather than being local to an injury or infection. It is long lasting and ongoing. Unlike acute inflammation, it is invisible, existing as inflammation in the blood chemistry, detectable only with certain lab tests. It causes havoc with the brain and body and is diametrically opposed to resilience.

Our lifestyle choices and habits directly correlate to our risk of systemic inflammation. Addressing the five elements of lifestyle will lower or eliminate the risk of chronic inflammation and its complications in a way that no medication or treatment can replace.

Diet. Poor nutrition is a major contributor to inflammation. A diet full of saturated fats, trans-fatty acids, refined carbohydrates, sugars, highly processed and deep-fried food are associated with higher production of pro-inflammatory molecules. Think of the perfect diet to create inflammation—fried chicken sandwich with French fries and a milkshake. On the other hand, a natural anti-inflammatory diet is loaded with vegetables and fruits, whole grains, plant-based and lean meat proteins, fish, and fresh herbs and spices. More on foods and resilience will be addressed in Part 2 of this book under DR1.

Exercise. A sedentary lifestyle creates a propensity for inflammatory diseases. Regular physical activity and exercise reduce inflammation. At the same time, exercise boosts chemicals in the body, such as endorphins, serotonin, and dopamine, that improve emotional well-being and decrease pain. There are many ways to create an effective plan to exercise, which are covered in detail in DR1.

Stress Management. Stress, whether from external events or internal thoughts, is a major trigger for systemic inflammation. Within moments of a stressful experience, inflammatory chemicals, such as cortisol, adrenaline, and cytokines, enter the bloodstream, affecting functions of the brain and body. In the brain, moodiness, impulsivity, and even depression can be the result. Stress blocks creativity and the ability to enjoy the present

moment. In the body it is experienced as pain and muscle tension. Chronic stress is synonymous with living in survival mode, as discussed in the previous chapter.

Sleep. Lack of sleep increases systemic inflammation, and systemic inflammation interferes with sleep. We all know this from experience—who isn't moody, unfocused and prone to aches when they are sleep deprived.

Addictive Toxins. Tobacco and most addictive substances, including alcohol and opiates, result in systemic inflammation. Repeated exposure can result in irreversible damage to the brain and, depending on the toxin, to the liver, lungs, GI tract and immune system.

> *"When you're hot, you're hot. And when you're not, you're not."* [ix]
> ~ Jerry Reed, American singer, songwriter

How do we know if we have excess systemic inflammation? Taking an honest look at the lifestyle list above is an excellent start. When any of these are significantly out of balance, systemic inflammation is likely. Another way to assess is to look at the harmony/disharmony ratio regarding physical and psychological well-being. Excessive body aches or presence of GI symptoms such as irritable bowel, indigestion or acid reflux are often indicators of inflammation. Susceptibility to colds and other infections may be a clue. Elevated blood sugars and increased LDL/VLDL "bad cholesterol" points to chronic inflammation. Moodiness, irritability, impulsivity, and depression may be manifestations of inflammation in the brain.

Take A Moment Activity
Assess Your Inflammation

Following is an informal self-assessment to help you gain insight into your current state of systemic inflammation.

Rate each of the following statements ranging from 1 to 5.

1	2	3	4	5
You totally disagree				You strongly agree

_____ I exercise or play sports at least three times per week.

_____ My diet generally consists of healthy foods.

_____ Sweets and fried foods are occasional rather than daily treats.

_____ I rarely feel stressed out.

_____ When something stressful happens I usually calm down quickly.

_____ I get an average of 7 hours of sleep per night.

_____ I drink no more than 2 servings of alcohol per day (males) or 1 serving per day (females).

_____ I walk at least 15 minutes daily (does not have to be all at once).

_____ I avoid cocaine and opiates for social or emotional purposes.

_____ I am rarely moody.

_____ I am rarely impulsive in words or actions.

_____ I feel rested when I wake up in the morning.

_____ **TOTAL**

Scoring

>30	30-39	40-49	50-60
High resilience risk	Moderate resilience risk	Resilient	Very resilient

Negative Thinking

"The world as we have created it is a process of our thinking. It cannot be changed without changing our thinking." [x]

~ Albert Einstein, German-born physicist

For the next 30 seconds do not think of a pink polka dot elephant… How's it going? When we say, "I don't want X to happen" or "I don't want to screw this up," we are having negative thoughts. The focus of the sentence is the X we don't want, and just like the pink polka dot elephant, our minds evoke the image, wanted or not. The problem is this: we are drawn toward what we think about and imagine. Adding to this, the negative thought evokes emotions consistent with the negative image. "I don't want to screw this up" creates the inner picture and felt sense of screwing it up. Anxiety and distress appear, making matters worse.

I learned this lesson when I was quite young. One day the summer I turned twelve, I was playing in the neighborhood park with friends We were running around and laughing. When we came upon a narrow creek, my friends easily jumped across the three-foot span. At that time in my life, I was not athletically inclined, and lacked self confidence in my physical abilities. As I approached the creek, the thought popped into my head: "Don't land in the creek; it would be embarrassing to land in the creek." Guess where my foot landed? My body followed the image my brain provided of landing in the creek. The word "don't" in the sentence created the fearful emotional tone that made failure more likely.

By chance or serendipity, months later I happened upon a book my father had been reading, "Psycho-Cybernetics" by Maxwell Maltz. I read about this phenomenon of negative thinking and how it sabotages our intentions. This was in the late 1960s. Dr. Maltz used a relevant analogy for that time—cybernetic missiles were in the news. They could self-correct once the target was set.

He explained that the mind is like that as well. It is extremely important to tell it exactly what your goal is, using images and visualization. Telling your mind where you don't want it to go is worse than useless. [xi]

Today the analogy would be GPS. Imagine getting into your car and turning on the GPS. When asked for the desired destination, you type in "not here." "Not here" is the negative input. It offers no useful information to find the destination. GPS needs positive details—city, street name and address. Our minds work amazingly similarly to GPS. The clearer and more detailed the destination we hold in our thoughts, the more likely we are to find our way there.

After reading Maltz's book, I returned to the park alone. I spent a few moments imagining jumping over the creek, feeling my foot land on the dirt and feeling good about it. Not surprisingly, when I did it again, my jump was successful!

Negative thinking generally presents in two ways: 1) outward projection of an unwanted outcome; and 2) inward projection of negative self-image.

Outwardly projected negative thinking, also known as negative expectancy, anticipates or expects what we don't want rather than what we do want. "Don't screw up this interview." "They won't like me." "Don't land in the creek." "I hope we don't lose the game." "Today will be as bad as yesterday." Each sentence conjures the image and feeling state of that which we wish to avoid. This makes it more likely that a negative outcome will occur.

Inwardly projected negative thinking sounds more like judgment or critique. We may hear this in our heads either as I or you statements. "You always screw things up." "I'll never succeed at anything." "I must be unlovable." "You idiot, why did you do that?" This language elicits self-guilt or shame. Done often enough, it creates hopelessness. While sometimes this inner verbal abuse is self-generated, often it is an echo of messages received by others during childhood.

In my work as a life coach, I frequently encounter this type of negative thinking. Whenever I first meet with a client or patient, I ask them to share their goals or desired outcomes. Often their responses only tell me what they do not want. "I need to get rid of this anxiety." "I don't want to be out of shape." "I can't live with this pain." "I have to stop using." These statements may initially sound like aspirations, but they are negative goals. They tell me nothing about the desired outcome. In GPS terms, the destination they are entering is "not here."

The consequences of negative thinking can be profound and far reaching. It is at the root of self-sabotage. It is the soil in which hopelessness grows and inertia blossoms. Resolve withers as it becomes more and more tempting to turn to numbing substances and behaviors to silence the critical voices and distressing images in our heads. After all, if I believe the voices in my head, I will never be loved, never be successful, never be happy. What's the use in trying? And if my suffering is inevitable, why not do anything that might give me a little relief, a little escape, even if just for a short while? In DR3 we will explore in detail how to turn this around, by creating positive goals with congruent, energizing emotions.

Disconnection

The consequence of living predominantly in survival mode combined with negative thinking is that we disconnect more and more from the very people and experiences that bring meaning and joy to our lives. We disconnect first from ourselves, numbing to avoid difficult emotions and internal criticism. We disconnect from others, isolating ourselves to avoid being seen for our perceived faults and failures. And we disconnect from the outer world, hopeless that we can find meaning, purpose or passion.

Disconnecting From Ourselves

"We cannot heal what we cannot feel."

~ John Bradshaw, American author

It is completely understandable that we would want to avoid the recurrent fear and anger arising from unresolved trauma and ACEs. Who wouldn't want to turn off the incessant shame and blame being spewed by our negative inner voices? It is natural to want to escape enduring grief, depression and anxiety. Avoiding painful emotions and thoughts may be a tempting idea, but suppression and numbing don't work. The effort simply pushes these energies into our tissues and subconscious, where they lurk and surface in destructive physical and mental ways. Numbing strategies, whether alcohol or drugs, food, sex, gambling, or internet surfing, may seem to work for a time; but our bodies and minds adapt to these over time with less and less relief. Also, numbing painful emotions also numbs our capacity to feel positive feelings like love and joy. Feelings contract in all directions when we numb ourselves. Resilient people learn to feel their feelings and observe their negative thoughts with compassion, allowing them to dissipate. The resilience strategies increase our capacity to be compassionate and accepting of our "perfectly imperfect" selves.

Disconnecting From Others

We humans are social creatures. Caring for and being cared for by others is required for a sense of wholeness. However, the inner wounds that we carry often compel us to isolate. We may feel unsafe in relationships. We may fear judgment for our imperfections or shame for our mistakes, wanting these to remain invisible. Anxiety and depression may make us feel incapable of tolerating social settings. Restoring resilience calls for us to reconnect with people who are supportive and uplifting, who accept us for who we are and encourage us to live our best lives. Some of us are fortunate to know loving people who help us reconnect. For others, restoring resilience is healing and letting go of unhealthy relationships and creating new, more positive connections.

During my years working in residential treatment, people often shared what was most important and restorative during their month or so stay. To my surprise, what stood out for them wasn't necessarily the therapies or classes. It was the experience of healthy relationships with others in treatment. For many it was the first time in their lives they could really share their true selves and feel seen and accepted. Listening, I knew that a key challenge for them as they returned home was to find and maintain this important sense of connection, belonging and sharing for a lifetime. For some, there were people waiting to embrace them. While others returned to relationships that were negative and draining or nonexistent. For them it would take a conscious effort to find and nurture new, healthy connections. Often this meant joining a support or recovery group, becoming part of a recovery group, becoming part of a learning community, volunteering, or attending a church/synagogue/mosque.

Disconnecting From the Universe

"Life is never made unbearable by circumstances, but only by lack of meaning and purpose." [viii]

~ Viktor Frankl, psychiatrist and author

As we lose our resilience, we often lose our sense of connection with the universe. For some this may be a loss of faith. Others may have given up on their dreams and aspirations. Many times, we become skeptics and dismiss our prior values and ethical standards.

Viktor Frankl was a psychiatrist and World War II Holocaust survivor. From his observations surviving Nazi imprisonment, he created a school of psychiatry called "Logotherapy," Latin for healing through meaning. His experiences and insights are recounted in his book, "Man's Search For Meaning," one of the most read books in the world.

Dr. Frankl proposes there are three ways that humans find meaning. Creative meaning occurs through our work, actions and deeds. Secondly, we find meaning through our experiences—taking in a sunset, enjoying a pet, listening to music. When neither creative nor experiential meaning is accessible, such as in a hospice bed or experiencing imprisonment, meaning can still be found through our attitude toward unavoidable difficulties and suffering.

In my medical and coaching work, I have found some people express discomfort with the words 'meaning' or 'purpose.' It reminds them of past negative experiences with organized religion. Meaning and purpose here do not refer to any imposed belief system. Finding our passion or doing what makes us feel fully alive are other ways to describe what we are talking about.

However we phrase it, restoring resilience calls us to rediscover who we are and our place in the world. I think writer Emily McDowell said it perfectly:

> 'Finding yourself' is not really how it works. You aren't a ten-dollar bill in last winter's coat pocket. You are also not lost. Your true self is right there, buried under cultural conditioning, other people's opinions, and inaccurate conclusions you drew as a kid that became your beliefs about who you are. 'Finding yourself' is actually returning to yourself. A remembering who you were before the world got its hands on you. [xiv][xv]

Restoring resilience is about the journey to find our way back home. Like Dorothy and friends in the Wizard of Oz, we are seeking wisdom (Scarecrow), courage (Cowardly Lion), and heart (Tin Man). In the end, Dorothy comes to understand that she always had the power to return to Kansas. In the next chapter we prepare to make a successful journey back home to resilience.

CHAPTER 4
The Secrets to Sustainable Resilience

If things start happening
Don't worry, don't stew
Just go right along
And you'll start happening too. [xv]

~ Dr. Seuss, American children's author

The previous chapters were about the problem of being and staying resilient. There is no doubt about the negative impact resulting from adverse childhood events, unresolved trauma, poor lifestyle choices and habits, negative thinking, and disconnection. I needed to paint a picture of the very real challenges that interfere with our well-being, but from this point forward, it is all about solutions.

Change can be scary. We often find ourselves out of our "comfort zone." We may fear having to go through hard times or pain; but "no pain, no gain" is apt here. While I imagine that seeking greater resilience was the reason you picked up this book, I also suspect that deep down you were aware that you would need to move

through some trepidation and/or resistance to be successful. This chapter is here to help you get ready for that journey.

Without further ado, here are the secrets to sustainable resilience:

- We must work on all Four Dimensions of Resilience (4DR).
- We're not expected to do any of this perfectly, just persistently.
- We all get off track sometime. When we do, we just pick ourselves up and continue.
- Sometimes it will feel like it isn't working. Wrong. If we persist, resilience will grow. If starting from a level of dysfunction or disorder on the resilience harmony/disharmony continuum, find professional support in the form of therapy, coaching, or a treatment program to augment the resilience strategies.

There are two ways you will experience positive change as you incorporate the 4DRs into your life. Let's call them linear and quantum change. Understanding and recognizing both forms of change will help you stay on track as you experience the ups and downs of the journey.

Linear refers to step by step change. When you decide to learn a foreign language, perhaps on day one you might learn five new words, and then five more words the next day. Keep this up over time, and vocabulary will grow in a linear type of fashion. Practice every day will eventually lead to fluency in your new language. Another example is starting an exercise regimen. Perhaps at first you can tolerate walking one mile at a slow pace. Little by little with repetition, endurance grows until you're walking three miles at a quick pace. This is a linear pattern of change. It is straightforward to see and measure success over time.

Quantum change, on the other hand, has a pattern that is very different. You try to change, and at first there appears to be no progress. Continued effort often leads to confusion or a sense of chaos. Then suddenly there is a shift or an 'aha' moment. This is the quantum change from one state to another. Before you is a new understanding or a new way of being, fully expressed.

As the story goes, this happened to Newton when the apple fell on his head. There was no linear development of his theory of gravity. First there was confusion, and the next moment there was clarity. Archimedes had his 'eureka' moment while getting into the bathtub. Suddenly he understood how to calculate displacement and density.

Quantum change is often described as transformational. For me, when I set out to write a song, I may struggle for hours, days or weeks without progress (the chaos phase). Then, in a flash, the entire melody presents itself to me. Authors describe the same phenomenon as 'writers block' until the breakthrough shows up. Quantum change often occurs while we are searching for meaning, purpose or passion. Perhaps there is linear preparation—reading books, making lists, attending classes. But the realization is often sudden, presenting as an insight, awareness or belief that comes into sharp focus. Some may describe this as a spiritual experience. Others may call it a "knowing" or "gift." People in addiction recovery often participate in linear, step-by-step actions to support abstinence. Sometimes months or years into their journey there is a moment when their cravings just vanish. Linear efforts, but then, quantum change.

Many of the strategies in part two of this book ask you to participate in activities that are repeated regularly, which often produce a generally linear kind of progress. Be assured that continued involvement will open the door to quantum change for you as well—realization, insight, understanding and breakthroughs.

The conceptual framework for this book came to me as a "Eureka" after many years of linear study and questioning around the matter of resilience. As I mentioned previously, I have spent my career pondering why some people bounce back from tragedy and trauma and others don't. Slowly, I have gathered pieces of information and effective approaches to help my patients and clients. But it came to me suddenly that all of the impediments to recovering well-being fall into four interdependent categories—the 4DRs. From that point on, when I worked with an individual who was stuck, who was in a state of inertia, there was always at least one of the 4DRs that was weakened or unaddressed. As inconspicuous, camouflaged, or opaque the block might be on the surface, literally everyone I worked with who was struggling was able to get back on course once the deficient dimension or dimensions were uncovered and addressed. Healing and recovery could progress. I came to see these 4DRs like the four tumblers of a combination lock—each tumbler needing to be dialed into its proper position for full resilience to be unlocked.

Before I leave the subject of linear vs. quantum change, I would like to emphasize that while quantum change is like a beautiful flower appearing one day seemingly out of nowhere, linear change is like tilling and weeding the soil. Our day-to-day work is tilling the soil, diligently practicing the strategies presented within the 4DRs. The appearance of the flower, the quantum change, is the eventual gift of our daily efforts. We can never forcefully pull the flower out from under the soil, nor force the petals to open with our hands. With patience and diligence, the flower blooms in its own good time.

For now, as we are about to embark on our resilience journey, it is helpful to create a basic vision of resilience goals. This will serve as our initial GPS system toward well-being and wholeness.

TAKE A MOMENT ACTIVITY
Setting the GPS

Complete the following sentences.

When my body is fully resilient:

    my body feels _____

    my body looks _____

    my body can _____

When I am emotionally resilient:

    my behavior is_____

    my mood is _____

When I am resilient in my thinking:

    I spend less time thinking about _____

    I spend more time thinking about _____

When my life is resilient:

    my work/career is _____

    my avocations/hobbies are _____

    my important relations are _____

I will know I have gotten what I need from this book when I:

_____

Each of the next four chapters details one of the Four Dimensions of Resilience:

Chapter 5 explores resilient biology—the lifestyle choices and habits needed for optimal health and energy.

Chapter 6 is about creating resilient emotional tone—the capacity to minimize time in survival mode and maximize time being present and creative.

Chapter 7 explains resilient thinking—the ability to think compassionately towards ourselves and to focus on positive goals.

Chapter 8 guides the way to resilient connections—connecting with ourselves, connecting in positive, supportive relationships, and connecting to the world through meaning, purpose and passion.

Chapter 9 puts it altogether, pointing the way forward to a lifetime of sustained resilience.

PART TWO:
Embracing the Four Dimensions of Resilience

CHAPTER 5
The First Dimension of Resilience: Resilient Biology

"Take care of your body. It's the only place you have to live."
~ Jim Rohn, American motivational speaker and author

"There are two types of habits: ones which comfort us, and ones which would be a comfort if we stopped." [xvii]
~ Catherine Pulsifer, American self-help author [xviii]

Our physical selves require care and maintenance to function in top form. As discussed in Section 1, the consequences of not taking good care of our bodies include premature aging, chronic disease, impaired mood and increased sensitivity to pain. The primary driver for all of these burdens is systemic inflammation (SI). So our job in the First Dimension of Resilience (DR1) is to create a lifestyle that normalizes this excess inflammation, thus avoiding or minimizing this resilience-draining burden.

DR1 requires focus and care within five aspects of lifestyle—diet, exercise, stress, sleep and toxins.

Addressing these will lower or normalize SI. Any incremental decrease in SI lowers the risk of what has been called "inflamm-aging," the effect of accelerated aging and chronic diseases due to excess inflammation. Addressing the five lifestyle components will not only lower inflammation, but also improve well-being in numerous other ways. For example, healthy lifestyle choices and habits release endorphins—natural pain relievers that block the perception of pain and increase feelings of well-being. They also increase serotonin, a neurotransmitter that enhances mood and protects against depression. Physical activity lowers stress by reducing excess adrenaline. When we add healthy and safe touch —people hugs, animal cuddling or a good massage—we boost a hormone called oxytocin. Oxytocin induces anti-stress-like effects, lowering blood pressure and cortisol levels. It improves pain tolerance, lowers anxiety and plays a role in social bonding. Reducing inflammation and boosting endorphins, serotonin and oxytocin help create a chemistry of happiness and well-being.

Patients and clients often ask me how they can know for sure whether or not they have excess inflammation. It's a reasonable question; but no matter the objective measure of inflammation, everyone needs to embrace a healthy lifestyle, either to reverse the risk factors of existing inflammation or prevent inflamm-aging from occurring in the first place. That being said, there are blood tests available which measure SI, directly or indirectly, for those seeking more objective testing. C-reactive protein (CRP) is the most common test. Not surprisingly, cardiologists often utilize this test to help assess risk factors for cardiovascular disease, a common and dangerous manifestation of inflamm-aging. Other tests point to SI indirectly. Hemoglobin A1C measures long term regulation of blood sugar levels. Hyperglycemia (elevated blood sugar) and diabetes are closely related to SI. Likewise, high levels of "bad" cholesterol, such as LDL and VLDL, are closely associated with SI. You can discuss these tests further with your healthcare provider.

Take A Moment Activity
How Am I Doing?

Rate each of the categories below from 1 to 10, with 1 "I am doing a poor job" and 10, an excellent job. In addition to diet, exercise, stress, sleep and toxins, I have added a play/leisure category, which overlaps with other categories and adds the element of healthy human and pet contact. Play and leisure activities reduce stress, provide physical activity, aid in sleep and enhance our sense of connection.

Rate each of the following statements ranging from 1 to 10.

| 1 | 2 | 3 | 4 | 5 | 6 | 7 | 8 | 9 | 10 |

I am doing poor   I am doing excellent

_____ Healthy Diet

_____ Regular Exercise

_____ Stress Management

_____ Quality Sleep

_____ Avoiding Toxins (tobacco, alcohol, opiates)

_____ Play/Leisure

_____ **TOTAL**

Scoring

10-30	31-45	46-60
Need serious changes	Would benefit from fine-tuning	Doing well

As I mentioned in Chapter 4, you are not expected to do any of this perfectly, just persistently. Success calls for a self-compassionate approach. Think journey, not destination, allowing for progress and back-sliding—"Fall down seven times, get up eight." ~ Japanese proverb.

Diet

> *"Let Food Be Thy Medicine,
> Thy Medicine Shall Be Thy Food."* [xix]
>
> ~ Hippocrates, Greek physician

Food for thought: there are foods that help us think better, boost mood, and keep our bodies healthy and strong. There are also foods that zap energy, make us moody, increase the risk of depression, and set us up for chronic and degenerative diseases. It is not my intention in this section to recommend a specific diet (such as Mediterranean, paleo, vegetarian, keto, Atkinson, intermittent fasting, etc.). Instead, I want to present basic information and a framework to help you shift your food choices in a healthier direction that is sustainable over time. It has been my experience that very few people successfully maintain an extensive, sudden dietary alteration, however healthy it may be.

Before I provide a list of health-promoting and health-impairing foods, let's look at dietary changes in the context of our lives. Many nutrition articles and books discuss diet as though food choices are simple and objective—that once you know which foods are good and bad, you can simply make the changes if you are so motivated. This is not at all my professional or personal experience. Food carries huge emotional and cultural significance for most people. There can be a great deal of internal pushback as we attempt to improve our food choices. My suggestions are to 1) make change slowly and gradually; and 2) select a strategy to monitor your eating. This approach is most likely to create lasting and sustainable improvement in what you eat.

1. Make change slowly. After looking at the list of helpful and harmful foods, try adding one good food while eliminating one bad food. That's it. Continue this simple adjustment daily until it feels easy. Then, in a week or two weeks when it's no big deal, add one additional good food daily and subtract one bad one. Slow it down if it seems unsustainable, and speed it up if it's easy.

2. Select a strategy to monitor eating. People who monitor their eating do better in sustaining positive change. Consider it a form of mindfulness. It doesn't matter so much how you monitor your diet, but some form of monitoring aids in success. Methods of monitoring include counting calories, weighing in daily, keeping a food diary, or following one of the professional monitoring programs such as Weight Watchers.

Resilience Boosting Foods

Vegetables are low in calories, but high in necessary nutrients. Most are a good source of dietary fiber, which aids digestion and helps control blood sugar.

Fruits also contain necessary nutrients and antioxidants that lower inflammation and boost immune function. Stick with the whole fruit rather than juices, which are higher in sugars and lose many nutrients and fiber when processed. If you struggle with blood sugar regulation or diabetes, you may need to limit fruit intake. Discuss with a knowledgeable healthcare provider.

Lean Proteins are needed to build and sustain muscles and organs. For meat eaters, consider poultry and fish as top contenders. Low-fat and nonfat and /nonfat dairy is a great source of protein, as are soybeans, lentils, beans, green peas, nuts and nut butters.

Healthy Fats, such as Omega3 fatty acids (from fish and flax) and mono-unsaturated oils (such as olive oil and nuts), have health-protecting qualities.

Complex Carbohydrates include foods such as whole grains, tubers and beans which have not been stripped of their nutrients and fiber through processing. These include 100% whole wheat breads, barley, quinoa, potatoes, oatmeal and beans.

Probiotics found in dairy products like yogurt and kefir or fermented foods like sauerkraut have an anti-inflammatory effect on the gut and the bodily system.

Water is essential for maintaining a normal temperature, lubrication of one's joints, and hydrating the skin. It also aids in digestion and kidney and brain function.

Resilience-Depleting Foods

Sugar, especially sugar added to foods, contributes to inflammation, weight gain, diabetes and fatty liver disease. Excess sugar intake is linked to increased risk of cardiovascular diseases, including heart attack and stroke.

Refined Carbohydrates are grains that have been processed to remove nutrients and fiber (think whole wheat or brown rice vs. white bread or white rice). These act much like sugar in the body and cause the same problems.

Deep Fried Foods are made with saturated and trans fats which promote plaque buildup in arteries (via inflammation). This increases risk of heart attack, stroke, obesity and other degenerative diseases. Try air frying or grilling instead.

Highly Processed Foods (think packaged, long shelf-life foods) typically contain too much added fat, sugar, and salt, and most contain problematic preservatives as well.

Red Meat is high in proteins and important nutrients. Some research suggests that high consumption may have health risks for cardiovascular disease and colon cancer. Perhaps best to limit frequency of consumption, choose grass fed sources, and stick with leaner cuts.

When you eat vegetables, lean protein, and complex carbohydrates at a meal and enjoy a fruit-based dessert, you are helping your body to be healthy and resilient. These foods are providing needed nutrients, plus adding antioxidant and anti-inflammatory effects to keep you younger and functioning at your best. Let me repeat here that little changes done slowly can have a positive, sustainable effect. Is fried chicken your favorite dinner? Consider reducing from daily to once or twice per week. Or give grilled chicken a try. Are you in the habit of drinking sugared sodas? Switch to iced tea or club soda. If that's too severe, mix soda with iced tea or club soda and slowly reduce the sweetened proportion. Let change be incremental, being mindful and gentle with your emotional responses to dietary changes. Appreciate the cultural and social meaning and connection of food in your life.

Take A Moment Activity

Making Dietary Changes

Select one problematic food that is a regular part of your diet and that you feel willing to change. Decide whether change means reducing how often you eat it or eliminating it. Select a healthy food to replace the old one. Keep a food diary and when the change becomes a new habit, select another food to reduce/eliminate and a new food to replace it. Here are a few common incremental changes:

- Fried chicken to grilled chicken
- Potato chips to cut-up carrots and/or celery
- Soda to iced tea or lemon water
- White bread to whole wheat or multi-grain bread
- Cookies to fruit
- Chop suey with white rice to brown rice
- Burgers 5 times a week to twice a week
- Pre-packaged breakfast tarts to low-fat yogurt

Exercise

> "My grandmother started walking
> five miles a day when she was sixty.
> She's ninety-seven now, and we don't know
> where the heck she is." [xix]
>
> ~ Ellen DeGeneres, American comedian

> "The only bad workout is the one that didn't happen."
> ~Anonymous

I am often asked what the best form of exercise is. My answer is simple—it's the one you like enough to keep doing. All forms of exercise are beneficial to health and longevity. While evidence suggests that a combination of aerobics and strength training offers the greatest boost to health, any activity you do is going to lower inflammation and increase well-being. So, start with something you enjoy doing. If no exercise is appealing in the beginning, pick the least onerous choice. The great news is that research confirms that any increase in exercise of any type has benefits. Walking for as little as 2 to 4 minutes has measurable health benefits!

Based on the research evidence, the sweet spot for most people for exercise is 30 to 60 minutes of moderate exercise three to five days per week, which averages about 150 minutes per week. By sweet spot, I mean the optimal amount of health benefit and risk reduction. Alternatively, the same benefit is derived from 75 minutes of vigorous exercise per week if health and fitness permit. [xx]

Moderate vs. Vigorous Exercise

Moderate exercise includes things like walking briskly (three miles per hour or faster, but not race-walking), water aerobics, bicycling slower than ten miles per hour on level terrain, doubles tennis, ballroom dancing and gardening. Vigorous workouts might be race-walking, jogging, swimming laps, singles tennis, dance aerobics, bicycling greater than ten miles per hour on hilly terrain, and hiking uphill.

Take A Moment Activity
How to Assess Moderate vs. Heavy Exercise

The simplest way to get a general idea about the level of your exercise intensity is the breath test. During moderate activity you can typically talk full sentences but not sing. Vigorous exercise restricts talking to a few words at a time.

A more precise way to calculate activity intensity requires some math:

220 minus your age typically represents your maximum heart rate. For a 50-year-old that means
220 - 50 = 170 beats per minute maximum heart rate.

Moderate exercise falls in the range of 64% to 76% of maximum. For our 50-year-old, moderate exercise would fall between 109 (.64x170) and 129 (.76x170) beats per minute by checking pulse or with an activity tracker or smartwatch.

Vigorous intensity activity falls between 77% and 93% of maximum, which for our 50-year-old example is 131 (.77x170) to 158 (.93x170) beats per minute.

TAKE A MOMENT ACTIVITY
Get Moving

Make a list of the exercises and physical activities you find most appealing.

1. _____

2. _____

3. _____

4. _____

5. _____

Decide if you want to focus on one activity or prefer to rotate amongst them. (Personally, I get bored when I repeat an activity too often, so I have a list of 5 activities from which I can pick depending on my mood and energy level.) Now literally book the activities and times in your calendar. If you have been sedentary, start low and slow, and allow yourself to build up slowly. If you have been physically active, consider moving toward the 150 minutes of moderate or 75 minutes of vigorous movement per week. Consult your healthcare provider if you haven't exercised before or plan a significant boost in activity.

Stress

> *"There cannot be a crisis next week.*
> *My schedule is already full."*[xxi]
>
> ~ Henry Kissinger, American diplomat

Stress and worry are a part of modern life. Stress, biologically, is a form of the fight and flight response, a low, medium or high-level activation of the sympathetic nervous system, which was discussed in Part 1 of this book. "Managing" stress is both an inward and outward job. Externally, we manage stress by reducing or eliminating stressors that are under our control to change, or by practicing self-care. Internally we manage stress by developing and practicing skills that reduce emotional distress and by altering negative thoughts that create cognitive distress. Emotional regulation is covered in Chapter 6 (DR2). Managing our thoughts is explored in Chapter 7 (DR3). Here, we explore strategies to deal with external stressors.

TAKE A MOMENT ACTIVITY
Assessing Stressors

All life stressors can be improved, either by making a change in things that we have control of or by shifting our attitude toward unavoidable stress.

What is the most stressful part of your work (whether that is career or family related responsibilities)? _____

Could you change this for the better, even a little bit? _____

If so, how? When? _____

_____

If not, how could you improve your self-care to better cope with the stress? _____

_____

Who is your most stressful relationship? _____

What about the relationship is stressful? _____

Do you and the other person both want this to improve?

_____

If yes, how? _____

If no, can you reduce or avoid time with this person? _____

If yes, how? _____

If no, how could you improve your self-care to better cope with the stress? _____

What is the most stressful aspect of yourself? (This could include physical health, negative/critical thinking, loneliness, etc.) _____

Is this in your power to change? If so, what action could you take to improve this aspect of yourself? _____

If not, how could you be more accepting and kind to yourself?_____

Rank these three types of stressors (career, relationship, self) from most severe to least.

1. _____

2. _____

3. _____

Think of the smallest, easiest action you could take to make a positive change related to your most severe stressor, either by changing external circumstances or enhancing self-care. Write down this action on a piece of paper and put it where you will see it daily. Try taking this small, gentle step this week. At the end of the week, assess if you were successful. If so, how does it feel? Choose another action for week two and repeat the process. If you weren't successful, what got in the way? How can you approach it differently the following week? Or maybe you should choose an action that is even easier for week two. Either way, keep going.

Sleep

Most of us require seven to nine hours of sleep per night to be at our best. For some of us it is a nightly battle. Worries and anxiety can intrude on the salience of darkness. Perhaps the TV is on to distract us and help us unwind from the day, interfering with sleep. Whatever the cause, inadequate sleep is felt the next day, as we fight drowsiness and fatigue, decreased mental focus and increased body aches. Much of this is due to increased systemic inflammation resulting from lack of restorative sleep. A good night's sleep, on the other hand, leaves us feeling rested and ready to face the day.

Tips to Improve Sleep

Manage Sleep Hygiene. Sleep hygiene refers to habits and practices which improve sleep.

These include:

- going to sleep and waking up at approximately the same time every day
- avoiding electronics (TV, computer, phone) in the bedroom
- abstaining from caffeine in the late afternoon/evening
- refraining from vigorous exercise in the late afternoon/evening

Create Life Balance. Arrange work and home obligations to allow time for enough sleep. Both careers and children can make this feel impossible, but choosing a life of resilience makes it imperative that we solve the puzzle. Commit to figuring it out. Discuss with your support system. Work with a life or time management coach if needed.

Natural Supplements May Be Helpful. Often-used sleep supplements include melatonin, chamomile, valerian, and theanine. Check out aroma therapy with scents, such as lavender, bergamot, or ylang ylang. Read about the benefits of these natural sleep aids and discuss them with a healthcare expert.

Calm the Nervous System. Worry and anxiety are the enemies of sleep. Deep breathing, meditation, or relaxing music are excellent tools to turn off the stress. Much more about that in Chapter 6 (DR2).

Seek Support From a Sleep Specialist. If natural sleep strategies aren't helping or you suspect a sleep abnormality, such as sleep apnea, consult with a medical professional to help you find answers and solutions.

> A brief note about recreational toxins. Everyone knows the health risks of tobacco smoking. I will just add that smoking results in systemic inflammation and is contrary to a highly resilient life. Likewise, excess alcohol creates an inflammatory state and over time results in organ damage and premature aging. Eliminate smoking and cut back or eliminate alcohol consumption. If unsuccessful on your own, seek medical care, therapy or addiction treatment.

The building blocks of DR1—a healthy lifestyle incorporating diet, exercise, stress management, and good sleep—create biological resilience. Without these foundational elements, we are not prepared to live a life of healthy resilience. We can deal with our past traumas and triggers (DR2); we can think positively (DR3); we can have meaningful connections with others and pursue our passion and purpose (DR4); but if we neglect our body's needs, we are creating a biology that sets us up for mood irritability, depression, pain, degenerative conditions, and accelerated aging.

CHAPTER 6
The Second Dimension of Resilience: Resilient Emotional Tone

"One is certain of nothing but the truth of one's own emotions." [xxii]

~ E.M. Forster, English novelist

As I researched quotes to place at the beginning of this chapter, I was struck that my concept of emotions seemed so different from that of many authors, poets and philosophers. Some wax prolific about how thought must prevail over feelings. Others view some emotions as bad and unworthy. Yet others seem to confuse judgments for feelings. For example, the statement, "I feel like he's a jerk" or "I feel like this is going to be a good day," are judgments that accompany an emotion. I have a different take on emotions. They convey messages and guidance. Anger tells us that something is getting in the way of what we want or is ignoring our boundaries. Fear conveys danger and an urge to flee. Sadness says we have lost something or someone precious.

Feelings of joy and peace are messages that our needs are being met and struggle is unnecessary. Love speaks of our sense of connection. Acknowledging and listening to these emotions give us wisdom and insight.

Survival Brain vs. Creative/Present Brain

The emotions of anger and fear arise in an evolutionarily old part of the brain, an area called the limbic system. Anger and fear are accurately called survival emotions. In order to survive a threat to self, anger calls us to fight and fear pushes us to flee. These emotions are instinctual, calling us to act before thinking. For simplicity let's just say that these two emotions are connected to the survival brain. Other emotional qualities such as love, joy, compassion, and curiosity arise from a network of areas in the neocortex, an evolutionarily newer region of the brain. These qualities allow us to be focused, creative and present in the moment. Let's call this the creative/present brain. Resilient emotional tone refers to how and when we spend time with the survival brain running the show versus the creative/present brain. This balance determines our sense of well-being and the extent to which we access and express our human potential.

Neither system is "bad." In fact, both are needed. Survival brain is needed to respond to immediate threats. Creative/present brain is needed for optimal self-expression, personal and professional success and our overall well-being. If only it was as easy as flipping a switch. But human beings, with our amazing capacity to think abstractly, experience many physically safe situations as threatening and dangerous; thus, the survival brain is activated, suppressing our creative/present brain just when creativity, compassion and presence would be most useful to us. We discussed this in detail in Chapter 2: survival brain experiences metaphorical threats wherein there is nowhere to run and no one to fight. There is only useless muscle tension, and the unproductive emotional suffering of anger and fear.

Jeff was a client who came to see me at the request of his wife, Joan. She had noticed that he had become increasingly agitated when he was driving in traffic, cussing and pressing the horn repeatedly. A few days before we met, Joan had been in the passenger seat when Jeff was cut off by another car. Jeff rolled down his window and began screaming at the other driver. When Jeff and I discussed what was going on for him during driving, he revealed that he had recently been "cut off" from a job promotion that he had worked hard for and rightly deserved. He was carrying resentment and felt stuck in his career. It became clear that traffic congestion was the metaphor for his work experience. Since he couldn't safely express his anger at work and didn't want to distress his wife at home, he held his anger in until it came out sideways on the road. When he was able to face his anger head on and talk out his situation, his driving returned to normal.

Restoring a Balanced Brain and Nervous System

The solution to our overactive survival brain is to actively take steps to train and manage our nervous system. To do so we need to focus on calming the survival brain, creating a space between the thoughts and beliefs underlying our metaphorical threats and activating the creative/present brain. The most effective and clinically proven way to do this is something I call brain training. Brain training includes various forms of mindfulness that are excellent for calming and creating mental spaciousness. Brain training also includes techniques and practices that enhance focus, creativity, mood and gratitude.

If you have no interest or desire to meditate, please don't be scared off by the word, mindfulness. The words meditation and mindfulness for some connote a spiritual, mystical, or new-age lifestyle. Mindfulness, as I refer to it in this book, is something much more specific and scientifically studied. Simply, it is the means of intentionally bringing awareness to the present moment. It turns out that any technique that draws our attention to "here-and-now" lowers activity of the survival brain and increases activity in the creative/present brain. It makes sense. Any thought that is stressful or represents a metaphorical threat is often based upon an unpleasant memory from the past or worry about what might happen in the future. Removing focus on the past or future and bringing it back to the here-and-now is what mindfulness does. Extensive research confirms its effectiveness. People who spend several minutes a day purposely focused on the present experience less stress, less pain, better mood, and lower blood pressure.[xxiii]

The classic mindfulness technique is to turn our attention to our breathing, something that is always happening right here and right now. On top of the mental focus, slow and deep breathing physiologically reduces activity in the survival brain and activates the creative/present brain. If you've tried breath-focused meditation and found it ineffective or unpleasant, there are countless other ways to focus on the present moment that accomplish the same goal of shifting from survival brain to creative/present brain. Activities that require our complete focus, such as repetitive exercise, gardening, and listening to music also allow us to practice mindfulness.

The important thing is to build some form of mindfulness practice into our daily lives. Just like physical exercise, we get better and stronger with repetition. And just like exercise, we lose our proficiency when we stop practicing regularly. It is not important to do it perfectly. There is a false belief that successful mindfulness means the mind is quiet. Not true. It is natural that thoughts and feelings arise—it's what the mind does. With mindfulness practice, we are continually returning our awareness to the breath or other point of focus when we become aware of the mind wandering.

The daily practice of mindfulness lowers our baseline stress, thus enhancing resilience. It also prepares us to respond more resiliently when bad things happen. Having a technique to calm ourselves and create space from our already activated negative thoughts and judgments is also important. That space allows us to avoid impulsive words or actions driven by the survival brain that can sabotage relationships, careers and well-being.

Mindfulness Changes Our Brains

Some years ago, Harvard researchers were studying the effects of meditation. They made some surprising revelations. Stemming from the lead researcher's own personal experiences seeking respite from the stresses of academic life, the research team decided to learn more about why meditation practices were helping. Incorporating functional magnetic resonance imaging (fMRI) to study the effects of meditation on the brain, the researchers found measurable brain changes that can be seen on scans as a result of meditating.[xxiv]

The fMRI imaging records brain activity during the scan. The research demonstrated that daily mediation not only calmed brain activity during the session, but also throughout the day. This marked the first time such changes had ever been objectively detected. The exciting news from this is that our brains can and do adapt to positive changes in lifestyle and habits. Studies, from the Center for Healthy Minds at the University of Wisconsin-Madison, discovered that our brains not only change, but that change can be measured; and we can chart new pathways in the brain simply with new ways of thinking.

If you are unsure how to start your practice, there are books as well as classes both online and in-person that can help you get going. Or you can simply set aside a few minutes every day to tune into your chosen here-and-now focus. I have developed what I call my **Seven Minute Power Brain Training Exercise**, which my coaching clients find simple and easy to follow. It is a series of seven one-minute processes designed to quickly induce mindfulness and relaxation, boost focus and creativity, as well as

enhance mood and a sense of well-being. Try the Seven Minute Power Brain Training Exercise in the Take a Moment activity below. You can also find a free audio version on my website, LernerForLife.com.

Take A Moment Activity
Seven Minute Power Brain Training Exercise

Complete five or six breaths for each step to approximate one minute, then proceed to the next. Get in a comfortable position, either sitting or lying down with eyes closed.

Step 1: 4/4/8 breathing. Inhale to a count of four, hold to a count of four, and exhale to a count of eight. Continue at your own comfortable pace.

Step 2: Body scan up and down. Pay attention to your feet as you start to inhale. Slowly scan your body attention upward—so you reach the top of your head as you complete your inhale. Exhale slowly as you reverse scanning from your head down to your feet.

Step 3: Body scan center out. In your mind, find the very center of your body. As you inhale expand your attention in all directions outward like a growing bubble until you are aware of your entire body—front, back, top, and bottom. Exhale slowly, shrinking the bubble of your awareness back to the center of your body.

Step 4: Three good things. While breathing slowly and deeply think of one good thing, big or small. With the next few breaths enjoy that thought. Now think of a second good thing and with the next few breaths appreciate that thought. Bring a third good thing to mind, and, with the next few breaths, savor that thought.

Step 5: Subtle smile. While breathing slowly and deeply add a subtle smile to your face.

Step 6: Act as if. While breathing slowly and deeply think of one thing that you would like to be true and imagine that it is fully and completely true right now.

Step 7: Follow the breath. Simply follow your breath in and out. If your awareness drifts, gently bring attention back to your breath.

Take A Moment Activity
Create Your Personal Daily Brain Training Routine

Maximizing your time in creative/present mode requires a daily practice. Now is the time to determine which here-and-now practices you will do and when you will do them. Training may include:

- Meditation practice, such as following the breath or focusing on a candle, sound or word
- Being present in nature
- Meditative music
- Mindful walking
- Seven Minute Power Brain Training Exercise
- Journaling

Now book time in your calendar, between 5-15 minutes, once or twice daily.

Techniques for Emotional Regulation
Exercise

Regular exercise is a great way to manage the responses that our minds and bodies naturally default to when we are stressed. This is a technique that overlaps with what I mentioned in the previous chapter on lifestyle. There I specifically discussed the benefit of exercise to reduce inflammation, but exercise also provides a positive effect on our nervous system. As we all know, the benefits of exercise are immense. It improves our health, our metabolism, our ability to relax, and so much more.

Just as aerobic exercise brings remarkable changes to our bodies, it has a unique capacity to provide both stimulation and calm, counter depression, and reduce stress. It has been verified in clinical trials that athletes benefit from exercise when challenged by anxiety and depression. Exercise also discharges the excess energy that is activated when we go into fight or flight mode; it imitates the movement the body wants to do—swimming, jogging, or running mimic flight; hitting a ball with a bat or golf club mimics fight. The release of energy that exercise provides us is very beneficial to restoring the balance in our nervous system.

Another potential benefit of exercise and being involved in sports is that it provides opportunities to enhance social connections (DR4). Exercising in solitude is also beneficial and can be part of a mindfulness practice. What is the best type of exercise? The exercise you keep doing because you enjoy it. Whether you prefer a vigorous workout, circuit training, weight training, walking, jogging, or just a simple 20-minute stroll, exercise can work wonders to clear the mind and reduce stress. [xxvi]

Journaling

Journaling can help us explore and sort out our difficult thoughts and emotions safely and mindfully. Keeping a journal has been known to help one to manage anxiety, reduce stress, and cope with depression. It offers a tangible way to improve mood by tracking problems, fears, and concerns that trigger difficult emotions so that we can begin to deal with them. It also provides an opportunity for positive self-talk. Over the past two decades, there has been a growing body of literature that has demonstrated that writing about traumatic events helps an individual deal with them, which benefits physical and emotional health. [xxvi]

In one study on expressive writing, college students were asked to write for 15 minutes on four consecutive days about "the most traumatic or upsetting experiences" of their entire lives. Those who shared their deepest thoughts and feelings in their journal reported they were healthier overall, with less sick days and fewer visits to doctors. Also, people recuperating from physical wounds have been known to heal faster by journaling. Another study found that regularly writing strengthens immune cells and decreases symptoms of diseases, such as asthma and rheumatoid arthritis. Plus, the effect of writing, which accesses your left brain (the analytical, verbal, and rational side of your brain), leaves your right brain free to create. It seems like the act of writing can remove mental blocks and allow us to use all our brainpower to better understand ourselves, others, and the world around us. [xxvii]

Self Soothe

What do you find soothing? Common answers include being in nature, taking a bath, playing with pets, listening to a favorite music genre, taking a brief nap, getting a massage, and aroma therapy. Make a list of what works for you. Pick one and treat yourself whenever you need some restoration.

Take A Moment Activity
Move and Soothe

Create your de-escalation plan to use any time you find yourself triggered into a survival fight/flight mode.

There are two aspects of de-escalation, Move and Soothe. Moving helps release the tension created in the body. Soothing helps to quiet the mind and return to the here-and-now. Choose which Move and Soothe practices you will turn to when you need to adjust your emotional tone.

Move: Create a list of three brief (1 to 5 minute) activities that help release body tension: examples include:

- Take a walk
- Do stretches, pushups, sit-ups or jumping jacks
- Punch the air, shake out your arms and legs
- Run in place
- Squeeze a stress ball

Soothe: Create a list of five easy to access experiences that you find soothing. Examples include:

- Get a hug
- Cuddle with your pet
- Sit in nature
- Listen to a favorite song
- Repeat a meaningful affirmation or prayer
- Take slow, deep breaths
- Inhale a calming aroma
- Remind yourself of something you are grateful for

Keep your *Move and Soothe list* with you at all times—on your phone or in your purse or wallet. Whenever you feel activated or stressed go through the list one by one, alternating between moving and soothing, until you feel yourself calming down.

Dealing With Unresolved Trauma

Unresolved trauma, whether developmental or adult based, complicates and interferes with our capacity to live in creative/present mode. Trauma sensitizes us to activate the survival brain quickly and intensely. If you know or suspect trauma is interfering with your resilience, there are effective treatments that reduce activating triggers and facilitate healing. Explore these with a trauma-trained doctor or therapist. Effective therapies include SE (Somatic Experiencing), EMDR (eye movement desensitization and reprocessing) and Cognitive Behavioral Therapy, among others. The strategies discussed in this chapter and this book remain important during treatment and enhance recovery even if one is already participating in trauma therapy.

The qualities of DR2—presence and creativity—allow us to minimize our fight/flight response in stressful times and more effectively return to a state of calm when we are already activated. Without DR2, we become easily overwhelmed with life, and resilience is stifled. We can change our lifestyle and live healthier (DR1); we can think positively (DR3); and we can have meaningful connections with others and pursue our passions (DR4). But if we live life in survival mode much of the time, feeling excessively anxious, stressed, worried, and angry due to unresolved traumas and triggers, we are literally exhausting our chances for real sustainable resilience.

In the next chapter, we explore the pattern of negative emotions and negative thinking and how to shift toward positive thinking, envisioning and goal setting. Implementing DR3 will help us create a vision and path toward our best life.

CHAPTER 7
The Third Dimension of Resilience: Resilient Thinking

"The mind is its own place, and in itself, can make a heaven of Hell, a hell of Heaven." [xxviii]

~ John Milton, English poet

"Man can alter his life by altering his thinking." [xxix]

~ William James, American Psychologist

The Third Dimension of Resilience (DR3) is about learning thought skills and growing "thought muscles" that support us in discovering and creating our best lives. Lacking these, our thoughts will tend to sabotage us through negativity, self judgment and hopelessness.

Resilient Thinking Principle #1:
The Mind Ignores Disqualifiers

When I first interviewed Zak, a 33-year-old marketing executive, I asked him what his coaching goals were. His immediate answer was to stop screwing up his career, avoid eating junk food, and to not feel so "down" all the time. My first thought was that Zak's thinking was filled with negative statements, "don't do's." I then asked Zak, if he wasn't screwing up his career, eating junk food, and feeling down, what would his life look like and feel like? There was a long pause. He was clear about what he didn't want, yet he had no detailed vision of what he did want instead. We had a long talk about negativity that continued for many weeks.

Zak had a habit of using self-talk directed at what he didn't like about himself or what he didn't want to happen: "don't screw up this presentation;" "don't eat the cookies;" "what's wrong with you that you always feel so down?" During our coaching sessions, I invited him to listen to his harsh and negative self-talk. This was the voice of his judge and critic, and it was draining him of the energy and enthusiasm he needed to create a satisfying life. His inner words, and the images that were evoked, made him feel hopeless and pessimistic. (Remember Chapter Three—don't think of a pink polka dot elephant; negative statements cause us to fail every time!). His homework was to catch his inner judge and critic, challenge negative thoughts and turn them around. If he didn't keep screwing up his career, what would he like his career to look and feel like? If junk food was eliminated, what would he be eating and how would his body feel? What would he feel like and what would he be doing in life if his down moods were no longer present? Unfortunately, Zak found this assignment silly and futile. I am sure his thought was, this isn't going to work. And he proved himself right!

The kind of thinking that Zak was stuck in entangles us in a web of negativity. We can become so immersed in this negativity that it becomes invisible, like the air we breathe. We miss the fact that "I just don't want to be miserable" is no goal at all. It's like getting into your car, turning on the ignition and typing "not here" into GPS. We need to activate our inner GPS—Goal Positive System—giving it detailed information about the desired destination or outcome. The greater the detail we give our thinking brain, the more effective our guidance system is at figuring out the path.

Resilient Thinking Principle #2:
The Golden Rule Applies to Ourselves

The Golden Rule invokes us to "Treat others just as you want to be treated." How do you want to be treated? Presumably, we all want to be treated with kindness, compassion, courtesy, in a forgiving, encouraging and uplifting manner. Nowhere does the Golden Rule suggest we not treat ourselves the same way. In fact, I propose that it is impossible to truly show kindness and compassion toward others until and unless we direct those same qualities toward ourselves. And yet, there is a harsh judge and critic inside all of us. It developed in childhood to help us survive the trials and tribulations of growing up. And if we were exposed to harsh criticism or abuse from parents, siblings, teachers, clergy, or peers, that voice may be particularly loud and dominant. It is the unfortunate perspective of our inner judge and critic that it must beat us up to motivate us to survive and prosper. The judge may speak in second person—"What's wrong with you? "Can't you do anything right?" Or the judge might speak in first person—"I don't deserve to be happy; I'll never find the job/relationship/happiness I want." The critic also judges our circumstances as well as other people: "They're never going to hire me for this job." "That person won't accept my invitation to go on a date." "He's a jerk." "She's incompetent."

This negative pattern and habit of thinking inevitably leads to hopelessness. We become the donkey who never gets the carrot but relentlessly gets the stick. Even if our harsh self-talk leads to useful action and outcome, we are blocked from enjoying it.

You could have done better. That A should have been an A+. You got lucky this time, but it can't last. Wait till they discover I'm a phony. Resilience cannot survive the endless chatter of negative self-talk, judgment, criticism, and expectation of bad outcomes. Hopelessness, intermittent or constant, is the inevitable result. Hopelessness whittles our resilience down to nothing. It leads us to a variety of questionable behaviors to temporarily numb our guilt and shame, and it feeds our brains lies that drag us down. Hopelessness only results in more hopelessness. For a chronically negative thinker, the world is dark and there is no light at the end of the tunnel, so why try to make it out of the tunnel at all?

Resilient Thinking Principle #3:
Positive Goals + Congruent Emotions = Action

When we imagine accomplishing a desired positive goal, we might expect it to evoke positive emotions—joy, satisfaction, peace, love, gratitude, etc. These congruent emotions provide the fuel or enthusiasm to act. So, it is vitally important that when we envision goals they also contain the desired feelings. However, sometimes the imagined goal elicits paradoxical emotions such as sadness, fear, guilt, shame, anger or anxiety. When these paradoxical emotions appear and further envisioning of the desired outcome does not displace them with positive feelings, it is indicative that there is a belief or negative self-judgment that is sabotaging the goal. It is imperative to identify and challenge this negative voice until the congruent emotions are accessed.

Jesse was one of those people who struggled with negative messaging and emotions. When I met her she was doing all the right things to get her life back on track. She was taking care of her physical health, practicing meditation, pursuing meaningful work, and repeating affirmations daily. Her most important affirmation was," I am worthy of love and attracting a loving partner." She couldn't understand why she kept choosing partners who were unsupportive or downright negative in the way they spoke and behaved toward her. I asked her to repeat her affirmation out loud. I looked at her vision board, filled with pictures of happy and loving couples. Then I asked how she felt saying those words and looking at those pictures. Her answer, "sad, hopeless." I explained that her vision and affirmation were only half of the equation. They were her "GPS," but her emotions made up the other half—the fuel. Sadness and hopelessness meant her emotional gas tank was on empty. We spent several sessions exploring the origins of these feelings which were essentially contradicting the positive vision, words, and pictures.

During one session, we did a visualization where I asked her how old she was when she first felt these sad and hopeless feelings. She sensed it was around age 13. I asked her to think back to that age and those feelings and allow any thoughts to come to mind. What appeared was a long-forgotten memory. She liked a boy who did not like her back. One day she overheard her girlfriends talking about her behind her back, saying how she wasn't pretty enough to be with Bill. She felt angry and hurt as the memory came into focus. Then another memory appeared, this time of her older brother making fun of her body as it was changing during puberty. She felt shame. Later in the session she imagined confronting her friends and then her brother, expressing and releasing the anger and shame she could not process at age 13. She felt empowered and was able to challenge the messages that were embedded within her psyche so many years ago. The following session she felt different as she recited her affirmation—grounded, confident, energized. She now felt worthy of the love she sought. She was able to move forward.

There are many people like Jesse who firmly hold onto beliefs that have ingrained themselves into their subconscious. Understanding where those beliefs come from is a revelatory journey to the past that is certainly worth taking.

Take A Moment Activity
Start the Process
Let's do this in real-time.

1. Identify a goal. This can be in any area of life—health, relationships, career, etc._____

_____

2. Activate your GPS (Goal Positive System). Imagine this goal already accomplished in as much detail as possible.

What do you see, hear, smell, feel, etc.?_____

What do you look like? _____

What is your posture? _____

How do you move?_____

What are you wearing?_____

What are you doing?_____

With whom? Where? When?_____

_____

3. Check for and replace any negative descriptors and flip them to positive. For example, if your goal is to not be sad, flip it to what you do want to feel. If your goal is to not be in a dead-end job, flip it to what kind of job you do want. Apply the GPS to positive goals only.

4. Check for congruence of your emotional response to the completed goal. If the emotions are positive you are on your way. If emotions are incongruent, find and challenge the negative self-talk, self-judgment or belief that creates sadness, guilt, shame or hopelessness. If positive you are on your way. If emotions are incongruent, find and challenge the negative self-talk, self-judgment or belief that creates sadness, guilt, shame or hopelessness. If you're stuck, ask yourself, "when did I first have this negative feeling state and revisit the story. Take time to heal the wound that created this judgment and negativity. Keep exploring until emotions congruent with your desire appear.

5. Write your GPS down with all the details or create a vision board with drawings and pictures from magazines.

Resilient Thinking Principle #4: Positive Vision and Goals Require Daily Reinforcement

Imagining and feeling good about a goal on a one-time basis will not sustain the process. It is important to revisit the goal daily, bringing in the multi-dimensional sensory vision along with the positive congruent emotions. In addition to reinforcing the desired outcome, this allows for natural modifications and evolution of goals along the journey.

Take A Moment Activity
Reinforcement Strategies

Try the following:

1. Ponder what you are grateful for about this goal. Research confirms that a daily practice of gratitude alters our temperaments to be less pessimistic and more optimistic.

2. Create an affirmation. An affirmation is a positive statement about who or what we want to be, written or said in the present tense as though it has already come to pass. Some examples are: "I am worthy of love." I attract and am attracted to people who are positive and compassionate. "I connect with others through my honesty and inner joy." I make the world better through my daily work." Create an affirmation that reflects who you are when your GPS is a reality. Repeat it multiple times daily.

3. Keep a journal. Write down your vision and goals. Include your thoughts, feelings, struggles and victories.

Overcoming Inertia

With your vision in place, the congruent emotions providing energy, and a daily practice of reinforcing and boosting the intention, action is a natural consequence rather than something forced. When action is stymied or difficult, it suggests one of four things:

Goal Is Too Vague. When a goal is vague or only partly defined, it is like trying to build a house using a sketch rather than blueprints. The challenge here is to take the time to clarify and focus the vision, or alternatively, to take a general step in the right direction to find out what is called for next.

Goal Was Created to Please Others. For positive goal setting to be most effective, it will come from within you, either as an expression of who you are or as an expression of your values and life purpose. Choosing a career to please parents, choosing to marry because that person fits cultural expectations, or getting in shape because someone else is body-shaming you are all examples of goals that are limited; and, even if they are reached, they will not bring the joy inherent to those that come from the heart.

Goal Feels Overwhelming. There are some goals we choose in life that may be huge in scope and require multiple steps or sub-goals to get there. If your goal feels overwhelming, break it down into its sub-parts. Rejoice in the completion of each small step rather than waiting until the whole thing is complete. A journey starts with a single step, and the whole pizza is eaten one bite at a time.

Hidden Negative Belief. If you have a well-defined goal that naturally comes from within you and for which the sub-steps are developed, and yet you struggle to move forward or sustain the effort, this suggests that negative thinking or self-judgment is sabotaging the process. Take a deeper look at your critical beliefs and negative inner voices. Go back to the section on shifting from negative to positive thinking and dig deeper into pattern interruption and challenging the message. If you still hit a wall, consider a coach or therapist to help you through.

Further Thoughts About Beliefs, Negative Thinking, and Self-sabotage

Because negative thoughts and beliefs play a huge role in interfering with the life we want to manifest it is worthwhile to explore this topic in greater depth. Most negative thoughts we never "hear" consciously. They typically show up as intermittent or persistent feeling states that rise up through our subconscious. It takes effort to catch the underlying messages. When difficult emotions present themselves that contradict your vision, look for the message that your inner self is trying to send you. Ask, what does this emotion want to tell me? If no answer comes to you, take a guess and move forward as though it's the correct answer.

Following are the feelings that interfere with taking effective action towards our goals. Consider the underlying message that the emotion is communicating. Ask yourself the related questions to gain clarity.

Fear. I am unsafe or may be harmed if I pursue this goal. Questions—What is it that I fear might harm me? Is this fear realistic or false? How do I best face or challenge this fear?

Anger. Something or someone is getting in the way of my desired goal or infringing on my personal boundaries. Questions—With whom or about what am I angry? Is this block real or imagined? How can I get past this block? (Options may include to stand up for myself, create a strategy to get around the blockage, forgive, or let go and choose another path.)

Sadness. I will never get what I want or need. It is hopeless. Questions—Is this true? Is it only a partial truth? What is the rest of the truth? Do I believe I do not deserve what I want? If so, is this voice coming from me or is it a message I received from someone else? How do I challenge this impeding belief?

Guilt. I have done something wrong. Questions—Is that true? If false, can I let go of this guilt? If true, can I own up to it, make amends and restore my integrity?

Shame. I am inherently bad. Questions—Where did this message come from? From whom? When did I first experience this feeling and what was happening in my life? How do I challenge this belief and love myself for the perfectly imperfect person I am?

We can learn at any point to become more sensitive, to understand our emotions, and to be more accepting of them. Take Victoria, someone I worked with in residential treatment. The first time we visited, she was unable to identify any emotions around her marriage other than she loved her wife Chloe. Clearly, however, the relationship was having problems and it was unlikely she had no feelings about that. During our work together I continued to encourage her to dig deeper. "When Chloe promises to be home by 6:00 pm and arrives at 7:30 pm, how do you feel?"

At first, she said she didn't know. I asked her to guess. Her guess was correct—angry. We practiced connecting emotions to events and actions and over time she began doing that on her own. A month later she could identify what her emotion was at any time, or, if she wasn't sure she would "guess"—and she always guessed correctly. That was the beginning of her ability to share her feelings with Chloe.

Negativity, Numbing Behavior, and Self-Sabotage

The combination of chronic negative thinking combined with negative survival emotions leads eventually to hopelessness. This negative one-two punch creates the myth, "I am miserable and I will always be miserable." Without a strong Four-Dimensional Resilience program in place, this misery leads to its corollary: "I would do anything to get a break from this suffering, even for a little while." While this type of thinking is typically not conscious, it can become very present and eventually lead to hopelessness. This inevitably leads to numbing behaviors. Numbing behaviors are using unhealthy substances or taking unhealthy actions to temporarily make the suffering go away. Any mind or mood-altering drug can be misused in this way. For many of these drugs, substance use disorder is the eventual consequence. Briefly, these substances are addictive because at first, they work. For a few hours the emotional pain fades, the anxiety lifts, and we can let loose and have fun or relax.

The problem is that our brains adapt over time, and we need more and more of the substance to get back that good feeling. Eventually it no longer makes us feel good, but we feel awful without it. This is addiction.

We can do the same thing with numbing behaviors. These behaviors often involve things that in and of themselves are good or neutral. People misuse sex, food, pornography, gambling, exercise, the internet, etc. as ways to numb away difficult feelings and circumstances.

Numbing is a dead end and sometimes a deadly strategy. It interferes with a healthy lifestyle. It leaves us out of touch with difficult emotions that need to be heard, acknowledged, and tended to. It leads to self-judgment and criticism as it impacts relationships, careers, and health. And it isolates us from the uplifting relationships and meaningful activities needed for a fulfilling life. If you struggle with numbing substances or behaviors and are unable to turn them around with the resilience strategies alone, please reach out for help.

Harnessing Our Thoughts

In summary, DR3 is the practice of shifting thought patterns from negative to positive, envisioning positive goals and outcomes and bringing them into reality.

The mind ignores disqualifying statements. Get in the habit of using positively-worded descriptors. Challenge and flip negatively stated goals.

The golden rule applies to all of us. For resilience to grow and goals to be achieved, it is imperative that we speak to and think kindly about ourselves.

Positive goals plus congruent emotions equals action. To create energy and enthusiasm around a goal, evoke congruent positive emotions. Challenge and resolve incongruent emotions.

Positive vision and goals require daily reinforcement. Get in the habit of reviewing goals and evoking their positive emotions daily. In addition to envisioning, boost the energy behind your goals with a gratitude practice, affirmations, and journaling.

Overcome goal inertia. Explore—is the goal is too vague? Was the goal created to please others? Does the goal feel overwhelming? Is there is a hidden negative belief or message resulting in self-sabotage?

Listen to your uncomfortable emotions. Honor them by learning their language and messages. Fear, anger, sadness, guilt and shame can help us move forward and heal if we listen to them with compassion and provide self-care for our needs.

Recognize numbing strategies and their underlying message of hopelessness. Our resilience requires us to challenge and replace them with healthier choices. Have the courage to seek help if needed.

Shifting from negative to positive and manifesting our vision and goals is an ongoing and lifelong process. We get better at it as we practice. Imagine that!

The qualities of DR3, a positive and benevolent mindset, direct our inner life of thought toward manifesting the outer life we want to create. Without resilient thinking, we are drawn into the trap of negative expectancy and negative goal setting, greatly increasing the likelihood of experiencing that which we fear. We can change our lifestyle and live healthier (DR1); we can deal with past traumas and triggers (DR2); we can have meaningful connections with others and pursue a life of meaning and purpose (DR4); but if we allow negativity to rule our thinking, we lack the affirming hopefulness and vision that gives us the energy and enthusiasm needed to sustain lasting resilience.

CHAPTER 8
The Fourth Dimension of Resilience: Resilient Connections

"A great fire burns within me, but no one stops to warm themselves at it, and passers-by only see a wisp of smoke." [xxx]

~ Vincent Van Gogh, Dutch painter

"Eventually everything connects—people, ideas, objects. The quality of the connections is the key to quality per se." [xxxi]

~ Charles Eames, American designer

Feeling connected is a basic human need. We are a social species. We mostly grow up in families, learn in schools, work in teams, and function within communities. Biologically, our resilience is enhanced through connection. A loving hug or safe touch lowers stress and metabolic inflammation while raising "feel-good" chemicals, such as oxytocin and serotonin. A growing body of research shows that individuals who perceive their lives as meaningful or purposeful live longer, healthier and happier lives

than those who do not. [xxxii] Achieving and sustaining resilience in the realm of connections requires three expanding circles of connection:

1. Connection to self (listening and caring for needs of the body and spirit).

2. Connection to others (healthy and uplifting interconnection with family, friends and society)

3. Connection to the universe (experiencing a sense of belonging, meaning or enthusiasm in the world)

Connection to Self

In times of low resilience, we tend to lose touch with ourselves. We often stop listening to or caring for the needs of the body (DR1)—good diet, regular exercise, stress management and adequate sleep. We find ourselves out of touch or unable to support our emotional needs (DR2)—instead spending more and more time in the stress and survival modes with prominent anger, fear, and sadness while struggling to find any sense of peace, contentment, curiosity, gratitude or presence. Our thinking (DR3) tends to shift toward negativity and away from hope, and we are prone to isolate from friends and family and lose our sense of purpose or meaning (DR4). Resuscitating our relationship with self is the first step in restoring resilient connections. Every healthy relationship begins with good listening, and the relationship to self is no exception. Mindfulness practice, focused breathing, or the Seven Minute Power Brain Training Exercise are all wonderful ways to listen with compassion to our emotions and the needs they convey.

Take A Moment Activity
Connecting to Emotions with Compassion

Try this exercise the next time you are feeling emotional pain. Sit quietly in a comfortable position. Gently place one hand over your heart and the other over your belly. Identify and name the emotion you are feeling (such as anger, fear, sadness, guilt or shame). Taking your time, speak the following sentences to the emotion as though it was your best friend.

- I'm sorry you're hurting.
- I care about you.
- I'm here for you.
- We'll get through this together.
- May you be happy.
- May you be healthy.
- May you be at peace.

Repeat any time you find yourself rejecting, suppressing or judging your feelings.

Connection to Others

During my career, I have had the honor of working at a few of the finest residential treatment programs in the country. What do patients at these places report as the best and most beneficial part of treatment? The most common response is striking—relationships developed with other patients. With all the top-quality therapies and treatments available at these facilities, the most healing experience is connecting to others. Because of the nature of the problems that bring people to these programs and the safe emotional environment that is created by the staff, patients often share their deepest pains and fears. They feel seen with compassion and acceptance, and in turn are more compassionate and understanding toward their fellow patients. Many lifelong friendships have been created in these environments.

There is simply no way to be resilient in isolation. The challenge is to create and sustain relationships that are uplifting and supportive. These types of friendships enhance our sense of well-being, safety and encourage us to be our best and truest selves. The flip side is true as well; relationships that feel critical, judgmental or disrespectful drain our resilience.

Sometimes we lose connections with others due to circumstances over which we perceive to not have control. Take Georgette for example. Prior to her mom developing dementia, Georgette described herself as very outgoing and social. She loved getting together with friends for dinner or meeting friends for a night out. However, when her mother's dementia reached the point when someone needed to be with her 24/7 for safety purposes, and Georgette was the only person willing and able to do so, she essentially had to give up her personal life to care for her mom. She did this from her heart, as her mother had been kind and giving her whole life, and Georgette wanted to return that love. Nevertheless, Georgette noticed she was slowly spiraling into depression.

After many months of caregiving, we met online and discussed her struggles. It was clear that she was totally committed to caring for her mother. It was also clear that she needed regular connections with her friends to feel whole inside. It was a conundrum that made her feel hopeless, but over time, Georgette was able to see ways to do both. She couldn't afford respite help, but it turned out that friends were happy to help with the caregiving and to create gatherings in her home on a regular basis as well. Joy and energy returned to Georgette, and she gladly cared for her mother for the remaining two years of her life.

Connection To the Universe

"For the meaning of life differs from person to person from day to day and from hour to hour. What matters, therefore, is not the meaning of life in general but rather the specific meaning of a person's life at a given moment." [xxxiii]

~ Victor E Frankl, Austrian psychiatrist

Connection to the universe explores questions like, "What is my place in the world?" "What kind of life do I choose to live?" "What are my values and ethics?" What gives me a sense of meaning or purpose?" What makes me feel fully alive?" So many of the people I have worked with in my career, whether seeking life coaching or help with recovery, reported at the beginning of the process that they felt they had lost themselves. They saw their healing as a path to find themselves again, to express their truest self, to find meaning, or to feel fully alive.

Meaning vs. Purpose vs. Passion

Whether we frame connection with the universe as meaning, purpose or passion is unimportant. What is important is that we find some way to be connected to life.

Meaning refers to the significance or importance we give to a person, experience or object. "This hug was very meaningful to me." "Sharing the sunset with you felt so meaningful." From this perspective we feel connected to the Universe when our lives are filled with meaningful experiences and significant relationships.

Purpose explores the "why" question. "I was born to sing." "I am alive to make sure other kids never have to suffer the way I did growing up." "My life is dedicated to serving… (God, my country, peace, those who suffer, etc.)." What is my purpose is a question that creates a struggle for some. It may feel like a burden or guilt, implying a sense of "should" or "must." The alternative is to ask—what makes me feel alive? It creates connection to the Universe through a passion for living.

Meaning, purpose and passion come from three sources according to Victor Frankl (who was mentioned previously). He called the First, "creative meaning," referring to purposeful work of any sort, from job or career to a valued hobby, to raising a family. The second, "experiential meaning" which is the inner experience of love, connection, or gratitude, such as appreciating nature or music or watching children play. Even when the capacity to experience creative or experiential meaning is taken from us, such as at times of illness or debility, we can access "attitudinal meaning," facing our unavoidable pain and suffering with a sense of courage and dignity. [xxxiv]

There are many people I have worked with who found their sense of meaning or passion through the very thing that hurt them most. I think of Katya, who was abused as a child, who developed a passion for working with children. There is James, in sustained alcohol recovery after several failed attempts, who can find nothing that makes him happier than helping another alcoholic find sobriety. Jillian was a victim of sexual assault, and after completing extensive trauma therapy, established a not-for-profit advocacy program for women going through similar experiences. Then there is Astrid, a highly successful executive, who used to work 100-hour weeks as a highly functioning workaholic, who finally found peace and balance in life by dedicating time to her family and returning to her childhood love of drawing. When we embrace and heal our wounds, that which caused us pain may be the very thing that heals our wounds, that which caused us pain may be the very thing that offers us direction and meaning.

Many others I have worked with found their sense of meaning and connection by looking through the lens of their childhood joy. Billy, recovering from major grief and loss, found comfort and reconnecting with his childhood love of, ventriloquism and puppetry. He now shares that joy by performing at a local children's hospital. Chandra spent all her free time as a child singing. As part of her healing from depression, she started taking voice lessons and now sings with her church choir, and even hopes to form a jazz and standards band someday. Growing up, Arthur, loved nothing more than his dog Skipper. After losing his business and life savings, he recently adopted a dog for the first time in decades, and finds peace taking her for long walks and playing fetch.

TAKE A MOMENT ACTIVITY
Who Am I?

Pick one of the following questions:

>   What is my purpose?

>   What are my most important values?

>   What makes me feel alive?

Grab paper and pen and for the next ten minutes write down your stream of thought around the question. Keep asking the question and write whatever comes to mind. It's okay to guess. Look for hints and clues. Think back to a time when purpose or values felt clear, or you felt excited to be alive. What created this inner sense? Try exploring these questions:

What did I love to do as a kid?_____

What were my unmet needs or wounds as a child that I would like to prevent others from experiencing?_____

What was the happiest time of my life?_____

Who is the most important person in my life?_____

What is the most important thing in my life?_____

What's the top item on my bucket list?_____

Revisit this exercise daily for one week. For week two, enhance your writings with your GPS (Goal Positive System discussed in Chapter 7.

The qualities of DR4—healthy connection with self, others and the world—offer a richness and depth to our lives no matter the circumstances. Without these connections we are left disconnected, isolated and adrift in life. We can change our lifestyle and live healthier (DR1); we can deal with past traumas and triggers (DR2); we can set positive goals (DR3); but if we are disconnected from ourselves, others, and the world, we miss the deep sense of belonging that sustains us through good times and bad and gives us reason to get up in the morning.

CHAPTER 9
Working The "Four Tumblers"

"Continuous effort—not strength or intelligence—is the key to unlocking our potential." [xxxv]

~ Winston Churchill, Prime Minister of the UK

The Four Dimensions of Resilience are represented by the metaphor of the four tumblers. Only when all four tumblers of a combination lock are in place does the system unlock to allow expression of our full potential. These 4DRs create an organic whole. Each requires the other in order to manifest its highest potential for healing and well-being. Resilient biology, resilient emotional tone, resilient thinking and resilient connections—these are the inseparable parts of the whole of human resilience.

This book has explored how it is that we lose resilience through circumstances, habits or choices, and the steps we can take to regain and optimize it for a lifetime. Using the information in this book along with the stories from my own life and those of my clients and patients, I hope you have an idea of where you are on the 4DR continuum and how to move toward higher and stronger resilience. It may seem like a lot, but I promise it is doable. So how do we put this all together and make it work? How do we get all the tumblers aligned? Let's start with a quick review of The Four Dimensions of Resilience.

DR1: Create Resilient Biology through adjusting lifestyle in small, sustainable ways. Little positive changes in the foods we choose and the exercise we do will have an anti-inflammatory effect that enhances mood and body comfort and reduces the risk of chronic mental and physical disorders. Taking time every day to relax and arranging life to get enough sleep will further enhance well-being.

The qualities of DR1—a healthy lifestyle incorporating diet, exercise, stress management, and good sleep—create biological resilience. Without these foundational elements, we are not prepared to live a life of healthy resilience. We can deal with our past traumas and triggers (DR2); we can think positively (DR3); we can have meaningful connections with others and pursue our passions or purpose (DR4); but if we neglect our body's needs, we are creating a biology that sets us up for mood irritability, depression, pain, and degenerative conditions.

DR2: Establish a Resilient Emotional Tone through daily brain training. Practice mindfulness in some form. Utilize conscious breathing to calm the nervous system once it is activated. Remind yourself every day of three things for which you are grateful. And determine to address any lingering trauma or emotional triggers through self-exploration and, if needed, professional support.

The qualities of DR2—presence and creativity—allow us to minimize our fight/flight/freeze response in stressful times and quickly return to a state of calm. Without this capacity, we become easily overwhelmed with life, and resilience is stifled. We can change our lifestyle and live healthier (DR1); we can think positively (DR3); we can have meaningful connections with others and pursue our purpose or passions (DR4); but if we live most of our life in survival mode, feeling excessively anxious, stressed, worried, and angry due to unresolved traumas and triggers, we are literally exhausting our chances for sustainable resilience.

DR3: Develop Resilient Thinking by catching and challenging negative beliefs and self-judgments. Use your GPS, Goal Positive System, to set positive vision and goals. Fuel your resolve by incorporating positive, congruent emotions.

The qualities of DR3—a positive, benevolent mindset—directs our inner life of thought toward manifesting the outer life we want to create. Without this skill we are drawn into the trap of negative expectancy and negative goal setting, greatly increasing the likelihood of experiencing that which we fear and descending into hopelessness. We can change our lifestyle and live healthier (DR1); we can deal with past traumas and triggers (DR2); we can have meaningful connections with others and pursue a life of meaning and purpose (DR4); but if we allow negativity to rule our thinking, we will lack the affirming hopefulness and vision that give us the energy and enthusiasm needed to sustain lasting resilience.

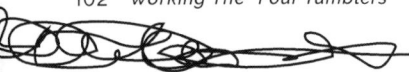

DR4: Engender Resilient Connections with self, others and the world by listening to and honoring the messages and needs conveyed by your emotions; establishing and nurturing positive, supportive relationships; and exploring your values, sense of purpose, or what makes you feel fully alive.

The qualities of DR4—healthy connections—offer a richness and depth to our lives no matter the circumstances. Without this connection with ourselves, loved ones, community, and the world at large, we are left feeling isolated and alone. We can improve our physical well-being through lifestyle changes (DR1); we can deal with past traumas and triggers (DR2); we can set positive goals (DR3); but if we live a disconnected life, without a sense of our place in the world, we miss that deep sense of belonging that sustains us through good times and bad and gives us reason to get up in the morning.

Moving Forward—The Cliff Notes

The Four Dimensions of Resilience benefit from a daily check-in. Ask yourself:

- Am I taking good care of my physical needs today?

- Have I taken time to be present and mindful?

- Am I thinking positively and staying focused on positive goals and vision?

- Am I listening to my feelings, connecting positively in relationships and with the world?

Fortunately, working the four tumblers is simpler than it seems. Exercise and stress management from DR1 directly support and mirror resilient emotional tone in DR2. Brain training from DR2 reinforces and boosts positive mind set in DR3. Creating positive vision and goals in DR3 ties in with finding meaning, purpose and passion in DR4. Connecting with self and others in DR4 aids stress reduction for DR1, supports a creative and present emotional tone for DR2 and reinforces a positive mindset for DR3. Round and round we go in an upward spiral, creating positive momentum.

There are three reminders I want to share before this book ends.

First, the best life gets is a state of harmony alternating with disharmony, pleasant times and difficult times. Living a life committed to resilience does not eliminate the pain of life. It does however, make it much more likely that you will rebound from difficult times more quickly and effectively.

Second, the strategies and actions we are committing to are mostly linear in nature, requiring daily practice. Quantum changes will happen in their own good time. Be patient and steadfast until the big, exciting and rewarding shifts come to you. They will!

Third, we need the resilience strategies and practices most urgently when we are least likely to be motivated and most likely to fall down. Be mindful and attentive to the urge to take a break or give up. Maybe even review this book in times of trouble and loss. There is a story about a meditation student sitting at the feet of the Master. The Master says, "You are required to meditate once every day." The student replies, "But Master, my life is too busy! I don't have time to meditate every day." The Master ponders for a moment and then responds, "Then it is required that you meditate twice every day." The moral of the story—when life is most difficult is when we most need to diligently engage with all of the resilience strategies. It is also the time we are most likely to feel the urge to let go of the good habits and self-care we have created for ourselves. Resilience in difficult times requires our ongoing commitment and action. It is worth the investment. You are worth the investment.

To help on your journey I invite you again to try my Seven Minute Power Brain Training Exercise; it is free for your use on my website, LernerForLife.com. You'll find it in the resources section, both written and audio versions. It is designed to reduce stress (DR1); enhance creativity and presence (DR2); encourage a positive mindset (DR3); and help you feel more connected (DR4).

And finally, please remember that resilience is an ongoing process, not a destination. Move forward with kindness and self-compassion. I wish you a fulfilling journey.

Jerry Lerner, MD

TAKE A MOMENT ACTIVITIES

Take A Moment Activity (Chapter 1)
Know Your Level of Resilience

Following is an informal self-assessment to help you gain insight into your current state of resilience.

Rate each of the following statements ranging from 1 to 5.

1	2	3	4	5
You totally disagree				You strongly agree

_____ I tend to bounce back quickly after stressful times.

_____ When I get upset, I generally calm down quickly.

_____ I am generally hopeful about life.

_____ I feel loved and supported.

_____ I ask for help when I need it.

_____ I have healthy and trusting relationships.

_____ My overall physical health is good.

_____ I choose healthy activities to decrease stress.

_____ I exercise at least 3 times per week.

_____ I generally feel well rested.

_____ My diet is generally healthy.

_____ I am compassionate toward myself.

_____ **TOTAL**

Scoring

>30	30-39	40-49	50-60
High resilience risk	Moderate resilience risk	Resilient	Very resilient

108 *Working The "Four Tumblers"*

TAKE A MOMENT ACTIVITY (CHAPTER 2)
Are You in Survival Mode?

Survival mode involves three core emotions: anger (fight), fear (flight) and numbness (freeze). Take a look at the words below that are associated with those core emotions How often are you experiencing these states? If your answer is rarely or occasionally, you are doing well. If your answer is often or most of the time, you are probably living predominantly in survival mode.

Core Emotion	Symptoms
Flight	Fear, anxious, worried, panicked, frightened, uneasy, apprehensive
Fight	Angry, annoyed, irritated, resentful, outraged, incensed, furious, impatient
Freeze	Numb, shutdown, disconnected, empty

Learning and practicing resilience skills will help restore a more balanced life. Keep reading.

Take A Moment Activity (Chapter 3)
Assess Your Inflammation

Following is an informal self-assessment to help you gain insight into your current state of systemic inflammation.

Rate each of the following statements ranging from 1 to 5.

1	2	3	4	5
You totally disagree				You strongly agree

_____ I exercise or play sports at least three times per week.

_____ My diet generally consists of healthy foods.

_____ Sweets and fried foods are occasional rather than daily treats.

_____ I rarely feel stressed out.

_____ When something stressful happens I usually calm down quickly.

_____ I get an average of 7 hours of sleep per night.

_____ I drink no more than 2 servings of alcohol per day (males) or 1 serving per day (females).

_____ I walk at least 15 minutes daily (does not have to be all at once).

_____ I avoid cocaine and opiates for social or emotional purposes.

_____ I am rarely moody.

_____ I am rarely impulsive in words or actions.

_____ I feel rested when I wake up in the morning.

_____ **TOTAL**

Scoring

>30	30-39	40-49	50-60
High resilience risk	Moderate resilience risk	Resilient	Very resilient

112 *Working The "Four Tumblers"*

Take a Moment Activity (Chapter 4)
Setting the GPS

Complete the following sentences.

When my body is fully resilient:

    my body feels _____

    my body looks _____

    my body can _____

When I am emotionally resilient:

    my behavior is_____

    my mood is _____

When I am resilient in my thinking:

    I spend less time thinking about _____

    I spend more time thinking about _____

When my life is resilient:

    my work/career is _____

    my avocations/hobbies are _____

    my important relations are _____

I will know I have gotten what I need from this book when I:

_____

Working The "Four Tumblers"

TAKE A MOMENT ACTIVITY (CHAPTER 5)
How Am I Doing?

Rate each of the categories below from 1 to 10, with 1 "I am doing a poor job" and 10, an excellent job. In addition to diet, exercise, stress, sleep and toxins, I have added a play/leisure category, which overlaps with other categories and adds the element of healthy human and pet contact. Play and leisure activities reduce stress, provide physical activity, aid in sleep and enhance our sense of connection.

Rate each of the following statements ranging from 1 to 10.

1	2	3	4	5	6	7	8	9	10

I am doing poor   I am doing excellent

_____ Healthy Diet

_____ Regular Exercise

_____ Stress Management

_____ Quality Sleep

_____ Avoiding Toxins (tobacco, alcohol, opiates)

_____ Play/Leisure

_____ **TOTAL**

SCORING

10-30	31-45	46-60
Need serious changes	Would benefit from fine-tuning	Doing well

As I mentioned in Chapter 4, you are not expected to do any of this perfectly, just persistently. Success calls for a self-compassionate approach. Think journey, not destination, allowing for progress and back-sliding—"Fall down seven times, get up eight." ~ Japanese proverb.

116 *Working The "Four Tumblers"*

Take A Moment Activity (chapter 5)
Making Dietary Changes

Select one problematic food that is a regular part of your diet and that you feel willing to change. Decide whether change means reducing how often you eat it or eliminating it. Select a healthy food to replace the old one. Keep a food diary and when the change becomes a new habit, select another food to reduce/eliminate and a new food to replace it. Here are a few common incremental changes:

- Fried chicken to grilled chicken
- Potato chips to cut-up carrots and/or celery
- Soda to iced tea or lemon water
- White bread to whole wheat or multi-grain bread
- Cookies to fruit
- Chop suey with white rice to brown rice
- Burgers 5 times a week to twice a week
- Pre-packaged breakfast tarts to low-fat yogurt

118 *Working The "Four Tumblers"*

Take A Moment Activity (chapter 5)
How to Assess Moderate vs. Heavy Exercise

The simplest way to get a general idea about the level of your exercise intensity is the breath test. During moderate activity you can typically talk full sentences but not sing. Vigorous exercise restricts talking to a few words at a time.

A more precise way to calculate activity intensity requires some math:

220 minus your age typically represents your maximum heart rate. For a 50-year-old that means
220 - 50 = 170 beats per minute maximum heart rate.

Moderate exercise falls in the range of 64% to 76% of maximum. For our 50-year-old, moderate exercise would fall between 109 (.64x170) and 129 (.76x170) beats per minute, or with an activity tracker or smartwatch.

Vigorous intensity activity falls between 77% and 93% of maximum, which for our 50-year-old example is 131 (.77x170) to 158 (.93x170) beats per minute.

Working The "Four Tumblers"

TAKE A MOMENT ACTIVITY (CHAPTER 5)
Get Moving

Make a list of the exercises and physical activities you find most appealing.

1. _____

2. _____

3. _____

4. _____

5. _____

Decide if you want to focus on one activity or prefer to rotate amongst them. (Personally, I get bored when I repeat an activity too often, so I have a list of 5 activities from which I can pick depending on my mood and energy level.) Now literally book the activities and times in your calendar. If you have been sedentary, start low and slow, and allow yourself to build up slowly. If you have been physically active, consider moving toward the 150 minutes of moderate or 75 minutes of vigorous movement per week. Consult your healthcare provider if you haven't exercised before or plan a significant boost in activity.

TAKE A MOMENT ACTIVITY (CHAPTER 5)
Assessing Stressors

All life stressors can be improved, either by making a change in things that we have control of or by shifting our attitude toward unavoidable stress.

What is the most stressful part of your work (whether that is career or family related responsibilities)? _____

Could you change this for the better, even a little bit? _____

If so, how? When? _____

_____

If not, how could you improve your self-care to better cope with the stress? _____

_____

Who is your most stressful relationship? _____

What about the relationship is stressful? _____

Do you and the other person both want this to improve?

_____

If yes, how? _____

If no, can you reduce or avoid time with this? _____

If yes, how? _____

If no, how could you improve your self-care to better cope with the stress? _____

What is the most stressful aspect of yourself? (This could include physical health, negative/critical thinking, loneliness, etc.) _____

Is this in your power to change? If so, what action could you take to improve this aspect of yourself? _____

If not, how could you be more accepting and kind to yourself?
_____

Rank these three types of stressors (career, relationship, self) from most severe to least.

1. _____

2. _____

3. _____

Think of the smallest, easiest action you could take to make a positive change related to your most severe stressor, either by changing external circumstances or enhancing self-care. Write down this action on a piece of paper and put it where you will see it daily. Try taking this small, gentle step this week. At the end of the week, assess if you were successful. If so, how does it feel? Choose another action for week two and repeat the process. If you weren't successful, what got in the way? How can you approach it differently the following week? Or maybe you should choose an action that is even easier for week two. Either way, keep going.

Take A Moment Activity (chapter 6)
Seven Minute Power Brain Training Exercise

Complete five or six breaths for each step to approximate one minute, then proceed to the next. Get in a comfortable position, either sitting or lying down with eyes closed.

Step 1: 4/4/8 breathing. Inhale to a count of four, hold to a count of four, and exhale to a count of eight. Continue at your own comfortable pace.

Step 2: Body scan up and down. Pay attention to your feet as you start to inhale. Slowly scan your body attention upward—so you reach the top of your head as you complete your inhale. Exhale slowly as you reverse scanning from your head down to your feet.

Step 3: Body scan center out. In your mind, find the very center of your body. As you inhale expand your attention in all directions outward like a growing bubble until you are aware of your entire body—front, back, top, and bottom. Exhale slowly, shrinking the bubble of your awareness back to the center of your body.

Step 4: Three good things. While breathing slowly and deeply think of one good thing, big or small. With the next few breaths enjoy that thought. Now think of a second good thing and with the next few breaths appreciate that thought. Bring a third good thing to mind, and, with the next few breaths, savor that thought.

Step 5: Subtle smile. While breathing slowly and deeply add a subtle smile to your face.

Step 6: Act as if. While breathing slowly and deeply think of one thing that you would like to be true and imagine that it is fully and completely true right now.

Step 7: Follow the breath. Simply follow your breath in and out. If your awareness drifts, gently bring attention back to your breath.

Take A Moment Activity (Chapter 6)
Create Your Personal Daily Brain Training Routine

Maximizing your time in creative/present mode requires a daily practice. Now is the time to determine which here-and-now practices you will do and when you will do them. Training may include:

- Meditation practice, such as following the breath or focusing on a candle, sound or word
- Being present in nature
- Meditative music
- Mindful walking
- Seven Minute Power Brain Training Exercise
- Journaling

Now book time in your calendar, between 5-15 minutes, once or twice daily.

TAKE A MOMENT ACTIVITY (CHAPTER 6)
Move and Soothe

Create your de-escalation plan to use any time you find yourself triggered into a survival fight/flight mode.

There are two aspects of de-escalation, Move and Soothe. Moving helps release the tension created in the body. Soothing helps to quiet the mind and return to the here-and-now. Choose which Move and Soothe practices you will turn to when you need to adjust your emotional tone.

Move: create a list of three brief (1 to 5 minute) activities that help release body tension: examples include:

- Take a walk
- Do stretches, pushups, sit-ups or jumping jacks
- Punch the air, shake out your arms and legs
- Run in place
- Squeeze a stress ball

Soothe: create a list of five easy to access experiences that you find soothing. Examples include:

- Get a hug
- Cuddle with your pet
- Sit in nature
- Listen to a favorite song
- Repeat a meaningful affirmation or prayer
- Take slow, deep breaths
- Inhale a calming aroma
- Remind yourself of something you are grateful for

Keep your *Move and Soothe list* with you at all times—on your phone or in your purse or wallet. Whenever you feel activated or stressed go through the list one by one, alternating between moving and soothing, until you feel yourself calming down.

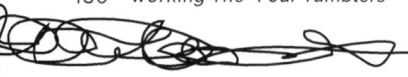

Take A Moment Activity (CHAPTER 7)
Start the Process

Let's do this in real-time.

1. Identify a goal. This can be in any area of life—health, relationships, career, etc._____

_____

2. Activate your GPS (Goal Positive System). Imagine this goal already accomplished in as much detail as possible.

What do you see, hear, smell, feel, etc?_____

What do you look like? _____

What is your posture? _____

How do you move?_____

What are you wearing?_____

What are you doing?_____

With whom? Where? When?_____

_____

3. Check for and replace any negative descriptors and flip them to positive. For example, if your goal is to not be sad, flip it to what you do want to feel. If your goal is to not be in a dead-end job, flip it to what kind of job you do want. Apply the GPS to positive goals only.

4. Check for congruence of your emotional response to the completed goal. If the emotions are positive you are on your way. If emotions are incongruent, find and challenge the negative self-talk, self-judgment or belief that creates sadness, guilt, shame or hopelessness. If positive you are on your way. If emotions are incongruent, find and challenge the negative self-talk, self-judgment or belief that creates sadness, guilt, shame or hopelessness. If you're stuck, ask yourself, "when did I first have this negative feeling state and revisit the story. Take time to heal the wound that created this judgment and negativity. Keep exploring until emotions congruent with your desire appear.

5. Write your GPS down with all the details or create a vision board with drawings and pictures from magazines.

Take a Moment Activity (Chapter 7)
Reinforcement Strategies

Try the following:

1. Ponder what you are grateful for about this goal. Research confirms that a daily practice of gratitude alters our temperaments to be less pessimistic and more optimistic.

2. Create an affirmation. An affirmation is a positive statement about who or what we want to be, written or said in the present tense as though it has already come to pass. Some examples are: "I am worthy of love." I attract and am attracted to people who are positive and compassionate. "I connect with others through my honesty and inner joy." I make the world better through my daily work." Create an affirmation that reflects who you are when your GPS is a reality. Repeat it multiple times daily.

3. Keep a journal. Write down your vision and goals. Include your thoughts, feelings, struggles and victories.

134 *Working The "Four Tumblers"*

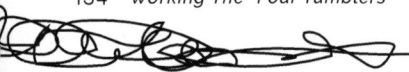

TAKE A MOMENT ACTIVITY (CHAPTER 8)
Connecting to Emotions with Compassion

Try this exercise the next time you are feeling emotional pain. Sit quietly in a comfortable position. Gently place one hand over your heart and the other over your belly. Identify and name the emotion you are feeling (such as anger, fear, sadness, guilt or shame). Taking your time, speak the following sentences to the emotion as though it was your best friend.

- I'm sorry you're hurting.
- I care about you.
- I'm here for you.
- We'll get through this together.
- May you be happy.
- May you be healthy.
- May you be at peace.

Repeat any time you find yourself rejecting, suppressing or judging your feelings.

Take A Moment Activity (Chapter 8)
Who Am I?

Pick one of the following questions:

> What is my purpose?
>
> What are my most important values?
>
> What makes me feel alive?

Grab paper and pen and for the next ten minutes write down your stream of thought around the question. Keep asking the question and write whatever comes to mind. It's okay to guess. Look for hints and clues. Think back to a time when purpose or values felt clear, or you felt excited to be alive. What created this inner sense? Try exploring these questions:

What did I love to do as a kid?_____

What were my unmet needs or wounds as a child that I would like to prevent others from experiencing?_____

What was the happiest time of my life?_____

Who is the most important person in my life?_____

What is the most important thing in my life?_____

What's the top item on my bucket list?_____

Revisit this exercise daily for one week. For week two, enhance your writings with your GPS (Goal Positive System discussed in Chapter 7.

GLOSSARY

AA. Alcoholics Anonymous: an international mutual aid fellowship dedicated to abstinence-based recovery from alcoholism through its spiritually inclined Twelve Step program. Related to other 12 step & anonymous groups such as Narcotics Anonymous (NA), Overeaters Anonymous (OA), Sex and Love Anonymous (SLA).

ACEs. Adverse Childhood Experiences: Refers to the cumulative effects on development related to repeated exposure to trauma, neglect, abuse, or loss.

Attitudinal Meaning. Finding meaning through our attitude toward unavoidable suffering.

Brain Training. Practices and exercises which improve various brain functions such as presence, calmness, creativity, gratitude and envisioning.

Creative Meaning. Expressing meaning through actions and choices.

Cytokines. A broad and loose category of small proteins in living organisms important in cell signaling, which have a significant effect on immune and inflammatory function.

Disease. Breakdown of mental/physical health from prolonged dysfunction.

Disharmony. Stressed, discontent, challenged.

Disintegration. Irreversible and progressive breakdown; death.

Disorder. Characterized by a clinically significant disturbance in an individual's regulation, or behavior. It is usually associated with distress or impairment in important areas of functioning.

Dysfunction. Living a suboptimal, less satisfying life.

Emotional Impulsivity. Reflexively acting out through words or deeds emotions such as anger and fear.

Experiential Meaning. Finding meaning through experiences; for example, enjoying a sunset or watching children play.

First Dimension of Resilience (DR1). Resilient biology. Refers to healthy lifestyle, addressing especially diet, exercise, stress management, and sleep.

Four Dimensions of Resilience (4DRs). The four aspects of wellness which as a whole creates optimal resilience.

Fourth Dimension of Resilience (DR4). Resilient Connections. Connection to self (being in touch with our emotions and needs); connection to others (positive and uplifting relationships); and connection to the world (sense of meaning, purpose of passion).

Harmony. At peace, content.

Harmony/Disharmony Continuum. Resilient living fluctuates regularly between harmony and disharmony. Lots of resilience is represented by a downward spiral from harmony to dysfunction, to disease, and finally to disintegration.

Inflamm-aging. Premature and accelerated aging due to systemic inflammation.

Linear Change. Step by step change.

Microaggression. A statement, action or incident regarded as an indirect or subtle act of discrimination against members of a marginalized group (race, class, ethnic, orientation, etc.)

Mindfulness. The practice or experience of being in the present moment; awareness of what is here and now.

Negative Expectancy. The anticipation or belief that something bad is going to happen.

Neocortex. Region of the brain, most recently evolved, which is the center for higher brain functions, such as perception, decision-making, and language.

Parasympathetic Nervous System (PNS). Parasympathetic nervous system (PNS) Part of the autonomic nervous system, which deals with "rest and digest" activities such as eating, sleeping, immune function and social interaction. When the PNS is dominant, it allows for "creative and present" mode of functioning.

Prefrontal Cortex. Located at the front of the neocortex, functions as a control center, helping to guide our actions, and therefore, this area is involved during emotion regulation. Both the amygdala and the prefrontal cortex are part of the emotion network.

Quantum Change. A sudden shift from one state to another. May be physical, spiritual or psychological.

Radical Acceptance. The act and skill of not fighting or denying reality, that helps people learn how to accept painful events, people, or aspects of their life.

Resilience. The capacity to recover quickly from difficulties.

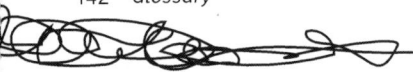

Second Dimension of Resilience (DR2). Resilient Emotional Tone. Refers to the practices that reduce time and intensity of survival mode in favor of increasing capacity to function in a creative and present mode.

Survival Brain. The part of the which is hyper-focused on survival through the activation of anger and/or fear and the initiation of flight or fight behaviors.

Survival Mode. The mode of brain functioning when fight, flight and/or freeze are Dominant. Survival mode suppresses activity in the neocortex resulting in loss of presence and creativity.

Sympathetic Nervous System (SNS). Sympathetic nervous system (SNS) Part of the autonomic nervous system, which drives survival activities, often called "fight and flight." Overactivity of the SNS is greatly involved with the loss of resilience.

Third Dimension of Resilience (DR3). Resilient Thinking. Refers to practices that diminish negative thinking and expectations while enhancing positive self-talk, envisioning, and goal setting.

REFERENCES

i. Kern, Jerome. & Fields, Dorothy. (1936). **Pick yourself up.**

ii. Mitchell, S. (1988). **Tao te ching.** Harper Collins.

iii. Jung, C. (1961). **The undiscovered self.** Signet/Mentor.

iv. Seyle, H. **It's not the stress.** Retrieved from www.goodreads.com/author/quotes/.

v. Whiteland, D. (2000). **Book of pages.** Pow Books.

vi. Frank, O. (1952). **Anne Frank: the diary of a young girl.** Doubleday & Company.

vii. Twain, M, **A habit cannot be tossed.** Retrieved from www.goodreads.com/author/quotes/.

viii. Twain, M. **Be careful about reading.** Retrieved from www.goodreads.com/author/quotes/.

ix. Reed, J. (1971). **When you're hot, you're hot.**

x. Einstein, A. **The world as we have created it.** Retrieved from www.brainyquote.com.

xi. Maltz, M. (1960). **Psycho-cybernetics.** Prentice-Hall.

xii. Bradshaw, J. (2010). **Healing the shame that binds you.** Simon and Schuster.

xiii. Frankl, V. (1946). **Man's search for meaning: an introduction to logotherapy.** Beacon Press.

xiv. McDowell, E. (2018). **Finding yourself** (Instagram Post).

xv. Seuss. (1990). **Oh, the places you'll go.** Harper Collins.

xvi. Rohn, J. **Take care of your body.** Retrieved from www.brewsterliving.org.

xvii. Pulsifier, C. (1998). Wings of wisdom: your daily guide to benefit from change, profit from failure, and design your own destiny. Anncath—Roby Books.

xviii. Hippocrates. Let food be thy medicine, thy medicine shall be thy food. Retrieved from https://www.brainyquote.com.

xix. Degeneres, E. My grandmother started walking. Retrieved from www.brainyquote.com.

xx. Henry Kissinger Quotes. Retrieved from www.quotescosmos.com/quotes/HenryKissinger-quotes-1.html.

xxi. Henry Kissinger Quotes. Retrieved from www.quotescosmos.com/quotes/HenryKissinger-quotes-1.html

xxii. Forster, E.M. One is certain of nothing. Retrieved from www.goodreads.com/author/quotes.

xxiii. www.sciencedirect.com/science/article/abs/pii/S0272735815000197

xxiv. https://news.harvard.edu/gazette/story/2018/04/harvard-researchers-study-how-mindfulness-may-change-the-brain-in-depressed-patients/

xxv. www.health.harvard.edu/staying-healthy/exercising-to-relax

xxvi. www.intermountainhealthcare.org/blogs/topics/live-well/2018/07/5-powerful-health-benefits-of-journaling

xxvii. www.apa.org/monitor/jun02/writing

xxviii. Milton, J. The mind is its own place. Retrieved from www.goodreads.com/author/quotes.

xxix. James. W. Man can alter his life. Retrieved from www.goodreads.com/author/quotes.

xxx. Van Gogh, V. A great fire burns within me. Retrieved from www.brainyquote.com.

xxxi. Eames, Charles. Everything eventually connects. Retrieved from www.brainyquote.com

xxxii. www.medicalnewstoday.com/articles/longevity-having-a-purpose-may-help-you-live-longer-healthier#Living-longer-and-healthier-with-purpose

xxxiii. Frankl, V. For the meaning of life differs. Retrieved from www.brainyquote.com

xxxiv. Frankl, V. (1946). Man's search for meaning: an introduction to logotherapy. Beacon Press.

xxxv. Churchill, W. Continuous effort. Retrieved from www.goodreads.com/author/quotes.

If you enjoyed reading
my book please share
your opinion with others
on Amazon.com.
I would love to hear what
you have to say and
greatly appreciate
your support.

ABOUT DR. LERNER

Jerry Lerner, MD is a double-boarded physician in Rehabilitation Medicine and Addiction Medicine, as well as a Certified Executive Coach. His expertise extends to the role resilience plays in wellness, integrative medicine, addiction, pain recovery, trauma, and executive effectiveness.

Following a long career in clinical care and administrative leadership, Dr. Lerner currently provides executive and life coaching, as well as resilience trainings (LernerForLife.com). He previously served at Sierra Tucson as Chief Medical Officer along with fulfilling roles as Director of the Licensed Professionals and Executives Program and Director of the Pain Recovery Program. He also served as consultant and trainer for The Meadows in the areas of Pain Informed Care and Resilience Recovery. Dr. Lerner has lectured extensively and has led workshops and trainings throughout the country on topics of resilience, pain, trauma and addiction.

Dr. Lerner enjoys thinking outside of the box, exploring leading edge approaches to wellness, resilience and recovery. He has a lifelong love of the arts; his first major in college was music and he remains an avid pianist and composer.

Made in the USA
Columbia, SC
14 February 2024